Application for Asylum Based Upon Gender Discrimination and Sexual Abuse

Legal Strategies and Human Rights Perspectives for Gender-Based Asylum Claims

Attorney Brian D. Lerner

LAW OFFICES OF
BRIAN D. LERNER
A PROFESSIONAL CORPORATION

ATTORNEY DRAFTED IMMIGRATION PETITIONS

By

Brian D. Lerner
Attorney at Law

Disclaimer and Terms of Use:

INTRODUCTION

There are a multitude of different immigration petitions and applications. They are complex and full of requirements. Obviously it would be best to hire an immigration attorney to best prepare the petitions and applications. However, this can certainly cost thousands of dollars.

The next best option is to get a sample of the petition written by an experienced immigration attorney. The samples cost a fraction of what would be charged by an immigration attorney. However, while the reader has to alter, amend and change the parts of the sample petition to reflect their actual situation, it is a fantastic roadmap for them to use. If the reader has purchased the entire petition or application, they will have real live samples of cover letters, forms, declarations, affidavits and the necessary exhibits to use. The samples come from real cases and the names of those clients have been redacted to protect the privacy of that person or corporation.

These are petitions and applications that have been drafted by an experienced immigration attorney with over 25 years of experience. Get the benefits of that experience without the costs.

ABOUT THE LAW OFFICES OF BRIAN D. LERNER

Brian D. Lerner has been a licensed attorney since 1992 and started the Law Offices of Brian D. Lerner, APC. The law practice consists of Immigration and Nationality Law and everything involved with and regarding immigration which includes citizenship, investment visas, family and employment visas, removal and deportation hearings, appeals, waivers, adjustment, consulate processing and all types of immigration and citizenship matters. Thousands of families have been reunited and/or permitted to stay in the U.S. and/or return to the U.S. because of the successful work of Immigration Attorney Brian D. Lerner.

This law office handles all types of immigration cases including family based and employment based. Immigration issues range from immigration court proceedings to trying to fix what paralegals may have done that was neither correct nor proper. Foreign nationals must have experienced lawyers admitted to practice law.

The Law Offices of Brian D. Lerner, APC handles cases arising from business visas, work permits, Green Cards, non-immigrant visas, deportation, citizenship, appeals and all areas of immigration. The Law Offices of Brian D. Lerner, APC does EB-5 Investor Visas, H-1B Specialty Occupation, L-1 Intracompany Transferee, E-2 Treaty Investor, E-1 Treaty Trader, O-1 Extraordinary Ability among others. Regarding immigrant visas for the Green Card, the firm does PERM and advanced degree PERM, Family Petitions, and ExtraordinaryAlien Petitions. In addition to affirmative petitions, the Law Firm represents people in people in deportation and removal hearings, including political asylum, withholding of removal, and convention against torture cases.

Brian D. Lerner has been certified as an expert in Immigration & Nationality Law by the California State Bar, Board of Legal Specialization since 2000 and has been recertified three times. He now passes on his decades of experience by allowing the Reader, Law Schools, Professors and other Immigration Attorneys to purchase sample petitions on every facet of Immigration Law.

TABLE OF CONTENTS

ABOUT ASYLUM BASED ON SEXUAL PREFERENCE

Asylum based on sexual preference is recognized under U.S. and international law as a legitimate ground for protection, falling within the broader category of persecution based on membership in a particular social group. Courts have consistently held that individuals who face persecution due to their sexual orientation, gender identity, or gender expression constitute a recognizable and distinct social group under asylum law. This recognition acknowledges that lesbian, gay, bisexual, transgender, and queer (LGBTQ+) individuals are often subjected to severe discrimination, violence, and systemic abuse in many parts of the world simply because of who they are or whom they love.

Applicants seeking asylum on this basis must demonstrate that they have a well-founded fear of persecution in their home country due to their membership in this social group. Such persecution may include physical violence, imprisonment, social ostracization, or denial of basic human rights. It may also encompass psychological trauma, coercive medical procedures, or laws that criminalize same-sex relationships or gender nonconformity. The U.S. asylum system, following international conventions such as the 1951 Refugee Convention and its 1967 Protocol, provides a pathway to protection for individuals whose governments are unable or unwilling to protect them from such persecution.

Over the years, numerous precedential decisions have reinforced that sexual orientation and gender identity are immutable characteristics — inherent to an individual and fundamental to their identity — and therefore qualify for protection under the category of "membership in a particular social group." This evolving body of case law has been essential in establishing that persecution based on sexual preference is not merely a matter of private discrimination but a violation of fundamental human rights.

The growing recognition of LGBTQ+ asylum claims reflects a global shift toward inclusivity and equality, though significant challenges remain. Many applicants face difficulties in proving their sexual orientation or gender identity in legal proceedings, often due to cultural stigma or fear of further exposure. Legal advocates play a critical role in presenting credible testimony, expert evidence, and country condition reports that substantiate the applicant's fear of persecution.

Ultimately, asylum based on sexual preference, gender discrimination, or sexual abuse underscores the intersection of human dignity, justice, and compassion within immigration law. It reaffirms that every person, regardless of sexual orientation or gender, has the right to live free from persecution and to seek refuge where their safety and identity are respected and protected.

ATTORNEY COVER LETTER

September 23, 2015

California Service Center
U.S. Citizenship and Immigration Services
24000 Avila Road, 2nd Floor, Room 2312
Laguna Niguel, CA 92677

> Re: **Application: I-589, Application for Asylum and for Withholding of Removal**
> **Applicant:** ███████████████
> **Country of Birth: The Bahamas**
> **Date of Birth: 03/31/1971**

Dear Officer:

██████████████ (hereinafter "Applicant"), through undersigned counsel, submits the following in support of his I-589, Application for Asylum and for Withholding of Removal:

Form:	Description:
G-28	Notice of Entry of Appearance As Attorney or Accredited Representative
I-589	Application for Asylum and for Withholding of Removal

Exhibit:	Description:
1.	Applicant's Declaration;
2.	Applicant's Birth Certificate;
3.	Applicant's Passport and I-94;
4.	Judge: Killing Was Justified To Avoid A Homosexual Act – Bahamas Local;
5.	"I Have Been Discriminated Against For My Sexuality" – The Tribune;
6.	Gay Cruise Passengers Met With Angry Protest In Bahamas – Bahamas B2B;
7.	Keith Bell's Deafening Silence – Bahamas B2B;
8.	History of Rainbow Alliance in The Bahamas - Theorizing Homophobias in the Caribbean;
9.	Government Against Gay Marriages – The Guardian;
10.	PM Against Gay Marriage – The Guardian;
11.	The March to Gay Marriage – The Guardian;
12.	Christian and LGBT Groups Have Brought The Battle For Gay Rights To The Caribbean – The Atlantic; and

13.   2014 Country Reports on Human Rights Practices: Bahamas -- U.S. Department of
        State.

I.
STATEMENT OF FACTS AND PROCEDURAL HISTORY

Applicant is a 44-year-old single male, native and citizen of the ▇▇▇▇▇▇, who last entered the United
States at Los Angeles, California on July 1, 2015, as a B-2 visitor for pleasure. **Exhibits 1-3.**
Applicant's I-589, including his written statement and supporting documents, contains evidence of the
following:

- Throughout his life in the Bahamas, Applicant was bullied, harassed and discriminated against
  because of his homosexuality. **Exhibit 1.**

- Serious human rights problems exist in the Bahamas including police abuse, corruption, an
  inefficient judicial system, and violence and discrimination based on gender, ethnic descent,
  sexual orientation and HIV status. **Exhibits 4-13.**

II.
ASYLUM UNDER SECTION 208 OF THE IMMIGRATION AND NATIONALITY ACT

Pursuant to section 208(b)(1) of the Immigration and Nationality Act (hereinafter "INA" or "Act"), the
Attorney General may grant asylum to any applicant who qualifies as a "refugee." The Act defines a
"refugee" as:

> "any person who is outside any country of such person"s nationality or, in
> the case of a person having no nationality, is outside any country in which
> such person last habitually resided, and who is unable or unwilling to
> return to, and is unable or unwilling to avail himself or herself of the
> protection of, that country because of persecution or a well-founded fear
> of persecution on account of race, religion, nationality, membership in a
> particular social group, or political opinion."

INS v. Cardoza-Fonseca, 480 U.S. 421, 428 (1987) (quoting INA § 101(a)(42)(A)); *see also* 8 C.F.R. §
1208.13; *Baghdasaryan v. Holder*, 592 F.3d 1018, 1023 (9th Cir. 2010) (quoting INA § 101(a)(42)(A)).

A.   Burden of Proof

An applicant bears the burden of establishing that he or she is eligible for asylum. 8 C.F.R. §
1208.13(a); *see also Halim v. Holder*, 590 F.3d 971, 975 (9th Cir. 2009); *Zhu v. Mukasey*, 537 F.3d
1034, 1038 (9th Cir. 2008); *Rendon v. Mukasey*, 520 F.3d 967, 973 (9th Cir. 2008); *Singh v. Gonzales*,
491 F.3d 1019, 1023-24 n. 2 (9th Cir. 2007). "An applicant alleging past persecution has the burden of
establishing that (1) his treatment rises to the level of persecution; (2) the persecution was on account
of one or more protected grounds; and (3) the persecution was committed by the government, or by
forces that the government was unable or unwilling to control." *Baghdasaryan v. Holder, supra.*

B.   Defining Persecution

The term "persecution" is not defined by the Immigration and Nationality Act. Ninth Circuit case law characterizes persecution as "an extreme concept, marked by the infliction of suffering or harm . . . in a way regarded as offensive." *Li v. Ashcroft*, 356 F.3d 1153, 1158 (9th Cir. 2004) (en banc) (internal quotation marks omitted); *see also Li v. Holder*, 559 F.3d 1096, 1107 (9th Cir. 2009). Threats of serious harm, particularly when combined with confrontation or other mistreatment and within a context of political and social turmoil or violence, may constitute persecution. *See, e.g., Mashiri v. Ashcroft*, 383 F.3d 1112, 1120-21 (9th Cir. 2004); *Kaiser v. Ashcroft*, 390 F.3d 653, 658 (9th Cir. 2004).

C.   Past Persecution

Once an applicant establishes past persecution, he is a refugee eligible for a grant of asylum, and the likelihood of future persecution is a relevant factor to consider in the exercise of discretion. *See Rodriguez-Matamoros v. INS*, 86 F.3d 158, 161 (9th Cir. 1996); *Kazlauskas v. INS*, 46 F.3d 902, 905 (9th Cir. 1995); *see also* 8 C.F.R. § 1208.13(b)(1)(i)(A). "If past persecution is established, a rebuttable presumption of a well-founded fear arises, 8 C.F.R. § 1208.13(b)(1), and the burden shifts to the government to demonstrate that there has been a fundamental change in circumstances such that the applicant no longer has a well-founded fear." *Tawadrus v. Ashcroft*, 364 F.3d 1099, 1103 (9th Cir. 2004) (internal quotation marks omitted); *see also Ahmed v. Keisler, supra*.

D.   Well-Founded Fear of Persecution

Even in the absence of past persecution, an applicant may be eligible for asylum based on a well-founded fear of future persecution. *See* 8 C.F.R. § 1208.13(b). A well-founded fear must be subjectively genuine and objectively reasonable. *See Ahmed v. Keisler, supra; Montecino v. INS*, 915 F.2d 518, 520-21 (9th Cir. 1990) (noting the importance of the applicant's subjective state of mind).

An applicant may demonstrate a well-founded fear by showing that he has been targeted for persecution. *See, e.g., Marcos v. Gonzales*, 410 F.3d 1112, 1119 (9th Cir. 2005); *Zhang v. Ashcroft*, 388 F.3d 713, 718 (9th Cir. 2004) (per curiam); *Melkonian v. Ashcroft*, 320 F.3d 1061, 1068 (9th Cir. 2003); *Lim v. INS*, 224 F.3d 929, 935 (9th Cir. 2000); *Mendoza Perez v. INS*, 902 F.2d 760, 762 (9th Cir. 1990).

Acts of violence against an applicant's family members and friends may also establish a well-founded fear of persecution. *See Korablina v. INS*, 158 F.3d 1038, 1044-45 (9th Cir. 1998); *see also Zhang v. Ashcroft, supra*; *Ingunna v. Ashcroft*, 374 F.3d 765, 769 (9th Cir. 2004) (persecution of family in Kenya); *Mgoian v. INS*, 184 F.3d 1029, 1035 n.4 (9th Cir. 1999) (violence and harassment against entire Kurdish Muslim family in Armenia); *Gonzalez v. INS*, 82 F.3d 903, 909-10 (9th Cir. 1996) (Nicaraguan family suffered violence for supporting Somoza); *Ramirez Rivas v. INS*, 899 F.2d 864, 868-69 (9th Cir. 1990) (granting relief where applicant was a member of a large politically active family that had been persecuted by Salvadoran authorities).

An applicant need not show that he or she will be singled out individually for persecution if the applicant establishes that there is a pattern or practice in his or her country ... of persecution of a group of persons similarly situated to the applicant on account of race, religion, nationality, membership in a particular social group, or political opinion. *See* 8 C.F.R. § 1208.13(b)(2)(iii); *see also Knezevic v. Ashcroft*, 367 F.3d 1206, 1213 (9th Cir. 2004) (evidence of a Croat pattern and practice of ethnically cleansing Bosnian Serbs); *Mgoian v. INS*, 184 F.3d 1029, 1036 (9th Cir. 1999) (pattern and practice of persecution of Kurdish Moslem intelligentsia in Armenia).

In the Ninth Circuit, a member of a "disfavored group" that is not subject to a pattern or practice of persecution may also demonstrate a well-founded fear. *See Kotasz v. INS*, 31 F.3d 847, 853-54 (9th Cir.

1994) (opponents of the Hungarian Communist Regime); *Tampubolon v. Holder*, 610 F.3d 1056, 1060 (9th Cir. 2010) (Christian Indonesians); *Ahmed v. Keisler*, 504 F.3d 1183, 1191 (9th Cir. 2007) (Bihari in Bangladesh); *Sael v. Ashcroft*, 386 F.3d 922, 927 (9th Cir. 2004) (Indonesia's ethnic Chinese minority); *El Himri v. Ashcroft*, 378 F.3d 932, 937 (9th Cir. 2004) (as amended) (stateless Palestinians born in Kuwait are members of a persecuted minority); *Hoxha v. Ashcroft*, 319 F.3d 1179, 1182-83 (9th Cir. 2003) (ethnic Albanians in Kosovo); *Singh v. INS*, 94 F.3d 1353, 1359 (9th Cir. 1996) (Indo Fijians).

E.   Nexus to the Five Statutorily Protected Grounds

For applications filed on or after May 11, 2005, the REAL ID Act of 2005, Pub. L. No. 109-113, 119 Stat. 231, created a new nexus standard, requiring that an applicant establish that "race, religion, nationality, membership in a particular social group, or political opinion was or will be *at least one central reason* for persecuting the applicant." INA § 208(b)(1)(B)(i) (emphasis added).

> "[A] motive is a "central reason" if the persecutor would not have harmed the applicant if such motive did not exist. Likewise, a motive is a "central reason" if that motive, standing alone, would have led the persecutor to harm the applicant. . . . [P]ersecution may be caused by more than one central reason, and an asylum applicant need not prove which reason was dominant. Nevertheless, to demonstrate that a protected ground was "at least one central reason" for persecution, an applicant must prove that such ground was a cause of the persecutors' acts."

Parussimova v. Mukasey, 555 F.3d 734, 741 (9th Cir. 2009).

1.   Mixed-Motive Cases

A persecutor may have multiple motives for inflicting harm on an applicant. For applications filed on or after May 11, 2005, § 101(a)(3) of the REAL ID Act provides that an applicant must establish that "race, religion, nationality, membership in a particular social group, or political opinion, was or will be *at least one central reason* for persecuting the applicant." INA § 208(b)(1)(B)(i) (emphasis added); *see also Sinha v. Holder*, 564 F.3d 1015, 1021 n.3 (9th Cir. 2009) (applying pre-REAL ID Act standard); *Parussimova v. Mukasey, supra*, ("[A] motive is a 'central reason' if the persecutor would not have harmed the applicant if such motive did not exist. Likewise, a motive is a 'central reason' if that motive, standing alone, would have led the persecutor to harm the applicant. . . . [P]ersecution may be caused by more than one central reason, and an asylum applicant need not prove which reason was dominant. Nevertheless, to demonstrate that a protected ground was 'at least one central reason' for persecution, an applicant must prove that such ground was a cause of the persecutors' acts.").

2.   The Protected Grounds

a.   Membership In A Particular Social Group

A particular social group "implies a collection of people closely affiliated with each other, who are actuated by some common impulse or interest." *Sanchez-Trujillo v. INS*, 801 F.2d 1571, 1576-77 (9th Cir. 1986) (stating that a family is a "prototypical example" of a social group, but young working class urban males of military age are not). "[A] 'particular social group' is one united by a voluntary association, including a former association, *or* by an innate characteristic that is so fundamental to the identities or consciences of its members that members either cannot or should not be required to change it," *Hernandez-Montiel v. INS*, 225 F.3d 1084, 1092-93 (9th Cir. 2000) (Mexican gay men with female sexual identities constitute a particular social group); *see also Perdomo v. Holder*, 611 F.3d 662, 669 (9th Cir. 2010) (BIA erred in rejecting "women in Guatemala" as a cognizable social group solely based on the broad nature of the group, without assessing 'innate characteristic' analysis); UNHCR's Guidelines on International Protection: Membership of a particular social group within the context of Article 1A(2) of the 1951 Convention and/or its 1967 Protocol relating to the Status of Refugees (HCR/GIP/02/02, 7 May 2002).

Sexual orientation and sexual identity can be the basis for establishing a particular social group. *Karouni v. Gonzales*, 399 F.3d 1163, 1172 (9th Cir. 2005) (holding that all alien homosexuals are members of a "particular social group."). *See also Castro-Martinez v. Holder*, 674 F.3d 1073, 1080 (9th Cir. 2011) (recognizing that "[h]omosexual men in Mexico can constitute a social group for the purpose of an asylum claim[,]" but concluding that petitioner failed to establish eligibility for asylum); *Boer-Sedano v. Gonzales*, 418 F.3d 1082, 1088-89 (9th Cir. 2005) (Mexican homosexual man forced to perform nine sex acts on a police officer and threatened with death persecuted on account of sexual orientation); *Hernandez-Montiel v. INS*, 225 F.3d 1084, 1092-93 (9th Cir. 2000) (Mexican gay men with female sexual identities constitute a particular social group), *overruled on other grounds by Thomas v. Gonzales*, 409 F.3d 1177 (9th Cir. 2005) (en banc), *judgment vacated by Gonzales v. Thomas*, 547 US 183 (2006); *Matter of Toboso-Alfonso*, 20 I. & N. Dec. 819, 822-23 (BIA 1990) (Cuban homosexual man established membership in a particular social group).

III.
APPLICANT IS ELIGIBLE FOR AND ENTITLED TO ASYLUM UNDER SECTION 208 OF THE ACT

In the present case, throughout his time in the ███████, Applicant was bullied, harassed and discriminated against because of his homosexuality. In elementary school, Applicant was routinely bullied and teased and called a "sissy" for being feminine and playing with girls. Applicant was also in several fights as a young boy, one in the 4th grade, where he was punched in the stomach and fractured a rib. This discrimination and harassment continued into middle school, where even teachers called Applicant derogatory names. More recently, at his 20th high school reunion, Applicant was verbally abused and publicly humiliated by a former classmate because of my sexuality, while others stood and watched. In addition, Applicant faced similar discrimination and harassment at various places of work. **Exhibit 1.**

Moreover, country condition materials establish that serious human rights problems exist in the Bahamas including police abuse, corruption, an inefficient judicial system, and violence and discrimination based on gender, ethnic descent, sexual orientation and HIV status. **Exhibits 4-13.**

As for sexual orientation, under ███████, it is not considered a basis for discrimination, and therefore there have been very few published records of discriminatory crime toward LGBT individuals. In fact, the only piece of legislation addressing the legal status of homosexuality exists in Section 16 of the *Sexual Offenses and Domestic Violence Act, 1991*, which criminalizes public same-sex activity between adults, and any sexual activity between an adult and a minor of the same sex, with a penalty of up to 20 years imprisonment. Furthermore, the age of consent for same-sex sexual activity is 18 while the age of consent for heterosexual partners in 16.

According to a 2014 report by the U.S. Department of State, "the 2006 Constitutional Review

Commission found that sexual orientation did not deserve protection against discrimination."

According Rainbow Alliance Bahamas (hereinafter "RAB"), a gay rights activist group, many homosexuals face discrimination in the work force, housing market, and in other instances of violent hate crimes. NGOs and other gay rights activist groups are allowed to freely operate in the Bahamas. However, they have not seen great success historically because of low membership rates and underwhelming protection and support from the community. In fact, in August 2014 a Pride weekend in Grand Bahama was nearly abandoned after organizers of the events reported receiving threats and in the end, only five (5) individuals participated. As a result, many Bahamian LGBT individuals presumably stay "closeted" out of fear of rejection or physical harm at the hands of their community.

Further, as a predominantly Christian country, the █████████ Christian Council (hereinafter "BCC") has presented a strong opposition to legalizing gay marriage. According to various local news reports, few churches in the area are willing to perform marriages for same sex couples, although the ceremony has no legal value. In response to the UN's encouragement to provide gay rights to LGBT citizens, the BCC released a statement condemning the "hidden agenda" of the gay rights movement which it fears "could eventually lead to gay marriage." Similarly, many well-known Bahamian political figures openly oppose the promotion of gay rights and do not consider it a "pressing issue."

Exhibits 4-13.

Accordingly, Applicant fears that he will be subjected to further threats, harm, or possibly tortured and/or killed if he is forced to return to the Bahamas. **Exhibit 1.**

Based on the foregoing, Applicant has established that he has been persecuted in the Bahamas on account of his membership in a particular social group and accordingly, that he is eligible for and entitled to asylum under section 208 of the Act. Because Applicant has established past persecution, he is presumed to have a well-founded fear of future persecution. *See* 8 C.F.R. § 1208.13(b)(1). However, should the Service determine that this presumption does not apply, Applicant has nevertheless established a well-found fear of future persecution (both objectively and subjectively) based on evidence that he has been targeted because of his homosexuality and current country conditions in the Bahamas. *See, e.g., Marcos v. Gonzales, supra; Zhang v. Ashcroft, supra; Korablina v. INS, supra; Gonzalez v. INS, supra; Ramirez Rivas v. INS, supra;* and **Exhibits 1-13.**

VI.
CONCLUSION

Based on the forgoing, Applicant is eligible for asylum pursuant to section 208 of the Act and therefore, respectfully requests that the Service approve his I-589.

Dated: September 23, 2015

Respectfully submitted,

Brian D. Lerner
Attorney at Law

FORMS

Notice of Entry of Appearance
as Attorney or Accredited Representative

Department of Homeland Security

DHS
Form G-28
OMB No. 1615-0105
Expires 03/31/2018

Part 1. Information About Attorney or Accredited Representative

1. USCIS ELIS Account Number (if any)

▶ [ ][ ][ ][ ][ ][ ][ ][ ][ ][ ][ ][ ]

Name and Address of Attorney or Accredited Representative

2.a. Family Name (Last Name): Lerner

2.b. Given Name (First Name): Brian

2.c. Middle Name: David

3.a. Street Number and Name: 3233 E Broadway

3.b. Apt. ☐ Ste. ☐ Flr. ☐ [ ]

3.c. City or Town: Long Beach

3.d. State: CA   **3.e.** ZIP Code: 90803

3.f. Province: [ ]

3.g. Postal Code: [ ]

3.h. Country: USA

4. Daytime Telephone Number: 5624950554

5. Fax Number: 5626088672

6. E-Mail Address (if any): blerner@californiaimmigration.us

7. Mobile Telephone Number (if any): [ ]

Part 2. Notice of Appearance as Attorney or Accredited Representative

This appearance relates to immigration matters before (Select only one box):

1.a. ☒ USCIS

1.b. List the form numbers

I-589

2.a. ☐ ICE

2.b. List the specific matter in which appearance is entered

[ ]

3.a. ☐ CBP

3.b. List the specific matter in which appearance is entered

[ ]

I enter my appearance as attorney or accredited representative at the request of:

4. Select only one box:

☒ Applicant   ☐ Petitioner   ☐ Requestor
☐ Respondent (ICE, CBP)

Information About Applicant, Petitioner, Requestor, or Respondent

5.a. Family Name (Last Name): ▬▬▬▬

5.b. Given Name (First Name): ▬▬▬▬

5.c. Middle Name: ▬▬▬▬

6. Name of Company or Organization (if applicable)

[ ]

Form G-28 03/04/15 N

Part 2. Notice of Appearance as Attorney or Accredited Representative *(continued)*

Information About Applicant, Petitioner, Requestor, or Respondent *(continued)*

7. USCIS ELIS Account Number *(if any)*

   ▶ [ ][ ][ ][ ][ ][ ][ ][ ][ ][ ][ ][ ]

8. Alien Registration Number (A-Number) or Receipt Number

   [ ]

9. Daytime Telephone Number

   [███████████]

10. Mobile Telephone Number *(if any)*

    [███████████]

11. E-Mail Address *(if any)*

    [███████████]

Mailing Address of Applicant, Petitioner, Requestor, or Respondent

NOTE: Provide the mailing address of the applicant, petitioner, or respondent. If the applicant, petitioner, requestor, or respondent has used a safe mailing address on the application, petition, or request being filed with this Form G-28, provide it in these spaces.

12.a. Street Number and Name [███████████]

12.b. Apt. ☒ Ste. ☐ Flr. ☐ [████]

12.c. City or Town [███████████]

12.d. State [CA] 12.e. ZIP Code [91602]

12.f. Province [ ]

12.g. Postal Code [ ]

12.h. Country

   [USA]

Part 3. Eligibility Information for Attorney or Accredited Representative

Select all applicable items.

1.a. ☒ I am an attorney eligible to practice law in, and a member in good standing of, the bar of the highest courts of the following states, possessions, territories, commonwealths, or the District of Columbia. *(If you need additional space, use Part 6.)*

   Licensing Authority

   [Supreme Court of California]

1.b. Bar Number *(if applicable)*

   [158536]

1.c. Name of Law Firm

   [Law Offices of Brian D. Lerner]

1.d. I *(choose one)* ☒ **am not** ☐ **am**

   subject to any order of any court or administrative agency disbarring, suspending, enjoining, restraining, or otherwise restricting me in the practice of law. If you are subject to any orders, explain in the space below. *(If you need additional space, use Part 6.)*

   [ ]

2.a. ☐ I am an accredited representative of the following qualified nonprofit religious, charitable, social service, or similar organization established in the United States, so recognized by the Department of Justice, Board of Immigration Appeals, in accordance with 8 CFR 292.2. Provide the name of the organization and the expiration date of accreditation.

2.b. Name of Recognized Organization

   [ ]

2.c. Date accreditation expires

   (mm/dd/yyyy) ▶ [ ]

Part 3. Eligibility Information for Attorney or Accredited Representative (continued)

3. ☐ I am associated with

[_____],

the attorney or accredited representative of record who previously filed Form G-28 in this case, and my appearance as an attorney or accredited representative is at his or her request.

NOTE: If you select this item, also complete **Item Numbers 1.a. - 1.b. or Item Numbers 2.a. - 2.c.** in **Part 3.** *(whichever is appropriate).*

4.a. ☐ I am a law student or law graduate working under the direct supervision of the attorney or accredited representative of record on this form in accordance with the requirements in 8 CFR 292.1(a)(2)(iv).

4.b. Name of Law Student or Law Graduate

[_____]

Part 4. Applicant, Petitioner, Requestor, or Respondent Consent to Representation, Contact Information, and Signature

Consent to Representation and Release of Information

1. I have requested the representation of and consented to being represented by the attorney or accredited representative named in **Part 1.** of this form. According to the Privacy Act of 1974 and DHS policy, I also consent to the disclosure to the named attorney or accredited representative of any record pertaining to me that appears in any system of records of USCIS, ICE or CBP.

When you (the applicant, petitioner, requestor, or respondent) are represented, DHS will send notices to both you and your attorney or accredited representative either through mail or electronic delivery.

DHS will also send the Form I-94, Arrival Departure Record, to you **unless** you select **Item Number 2.a.** in **Part 4.** All secure identity documents and Travel Documents will be sent to you (the applicant, petitioner, requestor, or respondent) unless you ask us to send those documents to your attorney of record or accredited representative.

If you do not want to receive original notices or secure identity documents directly, but would rather have such notices and documents sent to your attorney of record or accredited representative, please select **all applicable** boxes below:

2.a. ☐ I request DHS send any notice (including Form I-94) on an application, petition, or request to the business address of my attorney of record or accredited representative as listed in this form. I understand that I may change this election at any future date through written notice to DHS.

2.b. ☐ I request that DHS send any secure identity document, such as a Permanent Resident Card, Employment Authorization Document, or Travel Document, that I am approved to receive and authorized to possess, to the business address of my attorney of record or accredited representative as listed in this form. I consent to having my secure identity document sent to my attorney of record or accredited representative and understand that I may request, at any future date and through written notice to DHS, that DHS send any secure identity document to me directly.

3.a. Signature of Applicant, Petitioner, Requestor, or Respondent

3.b. Date of Signature *(mm/dd/yyyy)* ▶ 09/09/2015

Part 5. Signature of Attorney or Accredited Representative

I have read and understand the regulations and conditions contained in 8 CFR 103.2 and 292 governing appearances and representation before the Department of Homeland Security. I declare under penalty of perjury under the laws of the United States that the information I have provided on this form is true and correct.

1. Signature of Attorney or Accredited Representative

2. Signature of Law Student or Law Graduate

[_____]

3. Date of Signature *(mm/dd/yyyy)* ▶ 09/09/2015

Part 6. Additional Information

Use the space below to provide additional information
pertaining to **Part 3., Item Numbers 1.a. - 1.d.**

_____

Department of Homeland Security
U.S. Citizenship and Immigration Services

U.S. Department of Justice
Executive Office for Immigration Review

OMB No. 1615-0067; Expires 12/31/2016

I-589, Application for Asylum and for Withholding of Removal

START HERE - Type or print in black ink. See the instructions for information about eligibility and how to complete and file this application. There is NO filing fee for this application.

NOTE: Check this box if you also want to apply for withholding of removal under the Convention Against Torture. ☒

Part A.I. Information About You

1. Alien Registration Number(s) (A-Number) (if any)	2. U.S. Social Security Number (if any) N/A

3. Complete Last Name	4. First Name	5. Middle Name
▮▮▮▮▮	▮▮▮▮▮	▮▮▮▮▮

6. What other names have you used (include maiden name and aliases)?

7. Residence in the U.S. (where you physically reside)

Street Number and Name	Apt. Number
▮▮▮▮▮	

City	State	Zip Code	Telephone Number
N. Hollywood	CA	91606	▮▮▮▮▮

8. Mailing Address in the U.S. (if different than the address in Item Number 7)

In Care Of (if applicable):	Telephone Number
▮▮▮▮▮	

Street Number and Name	Apt. Number
▮▮▮▮▮	▮▮▮▮▮

City	State	Zip Code
▮▮▮▮▮	CA	91602

9. Gender: ☒ Male ☐ Female	10. Marital Status: ☒ Single ☐ Married ☐ Divorced ☐ Widowed

11. Date of Birth (mm/dd/yyyy) 03/31/1971	12. City and Country of Birth ▮▮▮▮ Bahamas

13. Present Nationality (Citizenship) Bahamas	14. Nationality at Birth Bahamas	15. Race, Ethnic, or Tribal Group Black	16. Religion Christian

17. Check the box, a through c, that applies: a. ☒ I have never been in Immigration Court proceedings.

b. ☐ I am now in Immigration Court proceedings.   c. ☐ I am not now in Immigration Court proceedings, but I have been in the past.

18. Complete 18 a through c.

a. When did you last leave your country? (mm/dd/yyyy) **07/01/2015**   b. What is your current I-94 Number, if any? ▮▮▮▮▮

c. List each entry into the U.S. beginning with your most recent entry. List date (mm/dd/yyyy), place, and your status for each entry. *(Attach additional sheets as needed.)*

Date	Place	Status	Date Status Expires
07/01/2015	Los Angeles, CA	B-2	12/31/2015
10/30/2014	Los Angeles, CA	B-2	
09/06/2013	Los Angeles, CA	B-2	

19. What country issued your last passport or travel document? Bahamas	20. Passport Number ER0126771	21. Expiration Date (mm/dd/yyyy) 01/15/2023
	Travel Document Number	

22. What is your native language (include dialect, if applicable)? English	23. Are you fluent in English? ☒ Yes ☐ No	24. What other languages do you speak fluently? N/A

For EOIR use only.	For USCIS use only.	Action: Interview Date: _____ Asylum Officer ID#: _____	Decision: Approval Date: _____ Denial Date: _____ Referral Date: _____

Part A.II. Information About Your Spouse and Children

Your spouse ☒ I am not married. (Skip to **Your Children** below.)

1. Alien Registration Number (A-Number) (if any)	2. Passport/ID Card Number (if any)	3. Date of Birth (mm/dd/yyyy)	4. U.S. Social Security Number (if any)
5. Complete Last Name	6. First Name	7. Middle Name	8. Maiden Name
9. Date of Marriage (mm/dd/yyyy)	10. Place of Marriage	11. City and Country of Birth	
12. Nationality (Citizenship)	13. Race, Ethnic, or Tribal Group	14. Gender ☐ Male ☐ Female	

15. Is this person in the U.S.?
☐ Yes (Complete Blocks 16 to 24.) ☐ No (Specify location):

16. Place of last entry into the U.S.	17. Date of last entry into the U.S. (mm/dd/yyyy)	18. I-94 Number (if any)	19. Status when last admitted (Visa type, if any)
20. What is your spouse's current status?	21. What is the expiration date of his/her authorized stay, if any? (mm/dd/yyyy)	22. Is your spouse in Immigration Court proceedings? ☐ Yes ☐ No	23. If previously in the U.S., date of previous arrival (mm/dd/yyyy)

24. If in the U.S., is your spouse to be included in this application? (Check the appropriate box.)

☐ Yes (Attach one photograph of your spouse in the upper right corner of Page 9 on the extra copy of the application submitted for this person.)

☐ No

Your Children. List **all** of your children, regardless of age, location, or marital status.

☒ I do not have any children. (Skip to Part A.III., **Information about your background.**)

☐ I have children. Total number of children: _____

(**NOTE:** Use Form I-589 Supplement A or attach additional sheets of paper and documentation if you have more than four children.)

1. Alien Registration Number (A-Number) (if any)	2. Passport/ID Card Number (if any)	3. Marital Status (Married, Single, Divorced, Widowed)	4. U.S. Social Security Number (if any)
5. Complete Last Name	6. First Name	7. Middle Name	8. Date of Birth (mm/dd/yyyy)
9. City and Country of Birth	10. Nationality (Citizenship)	11. Race, Ethnic, or Tribal Group	12. Gender ☐ Male ☐ Female

13. Is this child in the U.S. ? ☐ Yes (Complete Blocks 14 to 21.) ☐ No (Specify location):

14. Place of last entry into the U.S.	15. Date of last entry into the U.S. (mm/dd/yyyy)	16. I-94 Number (If any)	17. Status when last admitted (Visa type, if any)
18. What is your child's current status?	19. What is the expiration date of his/her authorized stay, if any? (mm/dd/yyyy)	20. Is your child in Immigration Court proceedings? ☐ Yes ☐ No	

21. If in the U.S., is this child to be included in this application? (Check the appropriate box.)

☐ Yes (Attach one photograph of your spouse in the upper right corner of Page 9 on the extra copy of the application submitted for this person.)

☐ No

Part A.II. Information About Your Spouse and Children (Continued)

1. Alien Registration Number (A-Number) (if any)	2. Passport/ID Card Number (if any)	3. Marital Status (Married, Single, Divorced, Widowed)	4. U.S. Social Security Number (if any)
5. Complete Last Name	6. First Name	7. Middle Name	8. Date of Birth (mm/dd/yyyy)
9. City and Country of Birth	10. Nationality (Citizenship)	11. Race, Ethnic, or Tribal Group	12. Gender ☐ Male ☐ Female

13. Is this child in the U.S. ? ☐ Yes (Complete Blocks 14 to 21.) ☐ No (Specify location):

14. Place of last entry into the U.S.	15. Date of last entry into the U.S. (mm/dd/yyyy)	16. I-94 Number (If any)	17. Status when last admitted (Visa type, if any)
18. What is your child's current status?	19. What is the expiration date of his/her authorized stay, if any? (mm/dd/yyyy)	20. Is your child in Immigration Court proceedings? ☐ Yes ☐ No	

21. If in the U.S., is this child to be included in this application? (Check the appropriate box.)

☐ Yes (Attach one photograph of your spouse in the upper right corner of Page 9 on the extra copy of the application submitted for this person.)

☐ No

1. Alien Registration Number (A-Number) (if any)	2. Passport/ID Card Number (if any)	3. Marital Status (Married, Single, Divorced, Widowed)	4. U.S. Social Security Number (if any)
5. Complete Last Name	6. First Name	7. Middle Name	8. Date of Birth (mm/dd/yyyy)
9. City and Country of Birth	10. Nationality (Citizenship)	11. Race, Ethnic, or Tribal Group	12. Gender ☐ Male ☐ Female

13. Is this child in the U.S. ? ☐ Yes (Complete Blocks 14 to 21.) ☐ No (Specify location):

14. Place of last entry into the U.S.	15. Date of last entry into the U.S. (mm/dd/yyyy)	16. I-94 Number (If any)	17. Status when last admitted (Visa type, if any)
18. What is your child's current status?	19. What is the expiration date of his/her authorized stay, if any? (mm/dd/yyyy)	20. Is your child in Immigration Court proceedings? ☐ Yes ☐ No	

21. If in the U.S., is this child to be included in this application? (Check the appropriate box.)

☐ Yes (Attach one photograph of your spouse in the upper right corner of Page 9 on the extra copy of the application submitted for this person.)

☐ No

1. Alien Registration Number (A-Number) (if any)	2. Passport/ID Card Number (if any)	3. Marital Status (Married, Single, Divorced, Widowed)	4. U.S. Social Security Number (if any)
5. Complete Last Name	6. First Name	7. Middle Name	8. Date of Birth (mm/dd/yyyy)
9. City and Country of Birth	10. Nationality (Citizenship)	11. Race, Ethnic, or Tribal Group	12. Gender ☐ Male ☐ Female

13. Is this child in the U.S. ? ☐ Yes (Complete Blocks 14 to 21.) ☐ No (Specify location):

14. Place of last entry into the U.S.	15. Date of last entry into the U.S. (mm/dd/yyyy)	16. I-94 Number (If any)	17. Status when last admitted (Visa type, if any)
18. What is your child's current status?	19. What is the expiration date of his/her authorized stay, if any? (mm/dd/yyyy)	20. Is your child in Immigration Court proceedings? ☐ Yes ☐ No	

21. If in the U.S., is this child to be included in this application? (Check the appropriate box.)

☐ Yes (Attach one photograph of your spouse in the upper right corner of Page 9 on the extra copy of the application submitted for this person.)

☐ No

Part A.III. Information About Your Background

1. List your last address where you lived before coming to the United States. If this is not the country where you fear persecution, also list the last address in the country where you fear persecution. *(List Address, City/Town, Department, Province, or State and Country.)*
   (NOTE: Use Form I-589 Supplement B, or additional sheets of paper, if necessary.)

Number and Street (Provide if available)	City/Town	Department, Province, or State	Country	Dates From (Mo/Yr)	To (Mo/Yr)
▊▊▊▊▊	Nassau	▊▊▊▊▊	Bahamas	12 2010	06 2015

2. Provide the following information about your residences during the past 5 years. List your present address first.
   (NOTE: Use Form I-589 Supplement B, or additional sheets of paper, if necessary.)

Number and Street	City/Town	Department, Province, or State	Country	Dates From (Mo/Yr)	To (Mo/Yr)
▊▊▊▊▊	N. Hollywood	CA	USA	09 2015	
	Burbank	CA	USA	07 2015	09 2015
	Nassau	New Providence	Bahamas	12 2010	06 2015
	Nassau	New Providence	Bahamas	02 1987	12 2010

3. Provide the following information about your education, beginning with the most recent.
   (NOTE: Use Form I-589 Supplement B, or additional sheets of paper, if necessary.)

Name of School	Type of School	Location (Address)	Attended From (Mo/Yr)	To (Mo/Yr)
▊▊▊▊▊	College	Oakes Field	09 1994	05 2011

4. Provide the following information about your employment during the past 5 years. List your present employment first.
   (NOTE: Use Form I-589 Supplement B, or additional sheets of paper, if necessary.)

Name and Address of Employer	Your Occupation	Dates From (Mo/Yr)	To (Mo/Yr)
▊▊▊▊▊	Clerical	11 1999	04 2015

5. Provide the following information about your parents and siblings (brothers and sisters). Check the box if the person is deceased.
   (NOTE: Use Form I-589 Supplement B, or additional sheets of paper, if necessary.)

	Full Name	City/Town and Country of Birth		Current Location	
Mother	SPENCE ▊▊	Nassau	Bahamas	☒ Deceased Nassau	Bahamas
Father	▊▊▊	Harbour Island	Bahamas	☒ Deceased Nassau	Bahamas
Sibling	▊▊▊	Nassau	Bahamas	☐ Deceased Nassau	Bahamas
Sibling	▊▊▊	Nassau	Bahamas	☐ Deceased Nassau	Bahamas
Sibling				☐ Deceased	
Sibling				☐ Deceased	

(NOTE: Use Form I-589 Supplement B, or attach additional sheets of paper as needed to complete your responses to the questions contained in Part B.)

When answering the following questions about your asylum or other protection claim (withholding of removal under 241(b)(3) of the INA or withholding of removal under the Convention Against Torture), you must provide a detailed and specific account of the basis of your claim to asylum or other protection. To the best of your ability, provide specific dates, places, and descriptions about each event or action described. You must attach documents evidencing the general conditions in the country from which you are seeking asylum or other protection and the specific facts on which you are relying to support your claim. If this documentation is unavailable or you are not providing this documentation with your application, explain why in your responses to the following questions.

Refer to Instructions, Part 1: Filing Instructions, Section II, "Basis of Eligibility," Parts A - D, Section V, "Completing the Form," Part B, and Section VII, "Additional Evidence That You Should Submit," for more information on completing this section of the form.

1. Why are you applying for asylum or withholding of removal under section 241(b)(3) of the INA, or for withholding of removal under the Convention Against Torture? Check the appropriate box(es) below and then provide detailed answers to questions A and B below.

I am seeking asylum or withholding of removal based on:

☐ Race   ☐ Political opinion

☐ Religion   ☒ Membership in a particular social group

☐ Nationality   ☒ Torture Convention

A. Have you, your family, or close friends or colleagues ever experienced harm or mistreatment or threats in the past by anyone?

☐ No   ☒ Yes

If "Yes," explain in detail:
1. What happened;
2. When the harm or mistreatment or threats occurred;
3. Who caused the harm or mistreatment or threats; and
4. Why you believe the harm or mistreatment or threats occurred.

> **Since I was a young boy, I have been bullied, harassed and discriminated against because of my homosexuality.**
>
> **Please see attached declaration and supporting documents.**

B. Do you fear harm or mistreatment if you return to your home country?

☐ No   ☒ Yes

If "Yes," explain in detail:
1. What harm or mistreatment you fear;
2. Who you believe would harm or mistreat you; and
3. Why you believe you would or could be harmed or mistreated.

> **For the reasons stated above, I fear that I will be harmed or mistreated if I am forced to return to the Bahamas.**
>
> **Please see attached declaration and supporting documents.**

2. Have you or your family members ever been accused, charged, arrested, detained, interrogated, convicted and sentenced, or imprisoned in any country other than the United States?

☒ No ☐ Yes

If "Yes," explain the circumstances and reasons for the action.

3.A. Have you or your family members ever belonged to or been associated with any organizations or groups in your home country, such as, but not limited to, a political party, student group, labor union, religious organization, military or paramilitary group, civil patrol, guerrilla organization, ethnic group, human rights group, or the press or media?

☒ No ☐ Yes

If "Yes," describe for each person the level of participation, any leadership or other positions held, and the length of time you or your family members were involved in each organization or activity.

3.B. Do you or your family members continue to participate in any way in these organizations or groups?

☒ No ☐ Yes

If "Yes," describe for each person your or your family members' current level of participation, any leadership or other positions currently held, and the length of time you or your family members have been involved in each organization or group.

4. Are you afraid of being subjected to torture in your home country or any other country to which you may be returned?

☐ No ☒ Yes

If "Yes," explain why you are afraid and describe the nature of torture you fear, by whom, and why it would be inflicted.

For the reasons stated above, I fear that I will be tortured if I am forced to return to the Bahamas.

Please see attached declaration and supporting documents.

Part C. Additional Information About Your Application

(NOTE: *Use Form I-589 Supplement B, or attach additional sheets of paper as needed to complete your responses to the questions contained in Part C.*)

1. Have you, your spouse, your child(ren), your parents or your siblings ever applied to the U.S. Government for refugee status, asylum, or withholding of removal?

☒ No ☐ Yes

If "Yes," explain the decision and what happened to any status you, your spouse, your child(ren), your parents, or your siblings received as a result of that decision. Indicate whether or not you were included in a parent or spouse's application. If so, include your parent or spouse's A-number in your response. If you have been denied asylum by an immigration judge or the Board of Immigration Appeals, describe any change(s) in conditions in your country or your own personal circumstances since the date of the denial that may affect your eligibility for asylum.

2.A. After leaving the country from which you are claiming asylum, did you or your spouse or child(ren) who are now in the United States travel through or reside in any other country before entering the United States?

☒ No ☐ Yes

2.B. Have you, your spouse, your child(ren), or other family members, such as your parents or siblings, ever applied for or received any lawful status in any country other than the one from which you are now claiming asylum?

☒ No ☐ Yes

If "Yes" to either or both questions (2A and/or 2B), provide for each person the following: the name of each country and the length of stay, the person's status while there, the reasons for leaving, whether or not the person is entitled to return for lawful residence purposes, and whether the person applied for refugee status or for asylum while there, and if not, why he or she did not do so.

3. Have you, your spouse or your child(ren) ever ordered, incited, assisted or otherwise participated in causing harm or suffering to any person because of his or her race, religion, nationality, membership in a particular social group or belief in a particular political opinion?

☒ No ☐ Yes

If "Yes," describe in detail each such incident and your own, your spouse's, or your child(ren)'s involvement.

4. After you left the country where you were harmed or fear harm, did you return to that country?

☒ No   ☐ Yes

If "Yes," describe in detail the circumstances of your visit(s) (for example, the date(s) of the trip(s), the purpose(s) of the trip(s), and the length of time you remained in that country for the visit(s).)

5. Are you filing this application more than 1 year after your last arrival in the United States?

☒ No   ☐ Yes

If "Yes," explain why you did not file within the first year after you arrived. You must be prepared to explain at your interview or hearing why you did not file your asylum application within the first year after you arrived. For guidance in answering this question, see Instructions, Part 1: Filing Instructions, Section V, "Completing the Form," Part C.

6. Have you or any member of your family included in the application ever committed any crime and/or been arrested, charged, convicted, or sentenced for any crimes in the United States?

☒ No   ☐ Yes

If "Yes," for each instance, specify in your response: what occurred and the circumstances, dates, length of sentence received, location, the duration of the detention or imprisonment, reason(s) for the detention or conviction, any formal charges that were lodged against you or your relatives included in your application, and the reason(s) for release. Attach documents referring to these incidents, if they are available, or an explanation of why documents are not available.

I certify, under penalty of perjury under the laws of the United States of America, that this application and the evidence submitted with it are all true and correct. Title 18, United States Code, Section 1546(a), provides in part: Whoever knowingly makes under oath, or as permitted under penalty of perjury under Section 1746 of Title 28, United States Code, knowingly subscribes as true, any false statement with respect to a material fact in any application, affidavit, or other document required by the immigration laws or regulations prescribed thereunder, or knowingly presents any such application, affidavit, or other document containing any such false statement or which fails to contain any reasonable basis in law or fact - shall be fined in accordance with this title or imprisoned for up to 25 years. I authorize the release of any information from my immigration record that U.S. Citizenship and Immigration Services (USCIS) needs to determine eligibility for the benefit I am seeking.

| Staple your photograph here or the photograph of the family member to be included on the extra copy of the application submitted for that person. |

WARNING: Applicants who are in the United States illegally are subject to removal if their asylum or withholding claims are not granted by an asylum officer or an immigration judge. Any information provided in completing this application may be used as a basis for the institution of, or as evidence in, removal proceedings even if the application is later withdrawn. Applicants determined to have knowingly made a frivolous application for asylum will be permanently ineligible for any benefits under the Immigration and Nationality Act. You may not avoid a frivolous finding simply because someone advised you to provide false information in your asylum application. If filing with USCIS, unexcused failure to appear for an appointment to provide biometrics (such as fingerprints) and your biographical information within the time allowed may result in an asylum officer dismissing your asylum application or referring it to an immigration judge. Failure without good cause to provide DHS with biometrics or other biographical information while in removal proceedings may result in your application being found abandoned by the immigration judge. See sections 208(d)(5)(A) and 208(d)(6) of the INA and 8 CFR sections 208.10, 1208.10, 208.20, 1003.47(d) and 1208.20.

Print your complete name.	Write your name in your native alphabet.
▆▆▆▆▆▆▆	▆▆▆▆▆▆▆

Did your spouse, parent, or child(ren) assist you in completing this application? ☒ No ☐ Yes *(If "Yes," list the name and relationship.)*

| _____ | _____ | _____ | _____ |
| *(Name)* | *(Relationship)* | *(Name)* | *(Relationship)* |

Did someone other than your spouse, parent, or child(ren) prepare this application? ☐ No ☒ Yes *(If "Yes," complete Part E.)*

Asylum applicants may be represented by counsel. Have you been provided with a list of persons who may be available to assist you, at little or no cost, with your asylum claim? ☒ No ☐ Yes

Signature of Applicant *(The person in Part A.I.)*

[_signature_]

Sign your name so it appears within the brackets

Date *(mm/dd/yyyy)* 09/09/2016

I declare that I have prepared this application at the request of the person named in Part D, that the responses provided are based on all information of which I have knowledge, or which was provided to me by the applicant, and that the completed application was read to the applicant in his or her native language or a language he or she understands for verification before he or she signed the application in my presence. I am aware that the knowing placement of false information on the Form I-589 may also subject me to civil penalties under 8 U.S.C. 1324c and/or criminal penalties under 18 U.S.C. 1546(a).

Signature of Preparer	Print Complete Name of Preparer
signature	Brian D. Lerner

Daytime Telephone Number	Address of Preparer: Street Number and Name		
(562) 495-0554	3233 E. Broadway		

Apt. Number	City	State	Zip Code
	Long Beach	CA	90803

Part F. To Be Completed at Asylum Interview, if Applicable

NOTE: *You will be asked to complete this part when you appear for examination before an asylum officer of the Department of Homeland Security, U.S. Citizenship and Immigration Services (USCIS).*

I swear (affirm) that I know the contents of this application that I am signing, including the attached documents and supplements, that they are ☐ all true or ☐ not all true to the best of my knowledge and that correction(s) numbered _____ to _____ were made by me or at my request. Furthermore, I am aware that if I am determined to have knowingly made a frivolous application for asylum I will be permanently ineligible for any benefits under the Immigration and Nationality Act, and that I may not avoid a frivolous finding simply because someone advised me to provide false information in my asylum application.

Signed and sworn to before me by the above named applicant on:

_____
Signature of Applicant

_____
Date *(mm/dd/yyyy)*

_____
Write Your Name in Your Native Alphabet

_____
Signature of Asylum Officer

Part G. To Be Completed at Removal Hearing, if Applicable

NOTE: *You will be asked to complete this Part when you appear before an immigration judge of the U.S. Department of Justice, Executive Office for Immigration Review (EOIR), for a hearing.*

I swear (affirm) that I know the contents of this application that I am signing, including the attached documents and supplements, that they are ☐ all true or ☐ not all true to the best of my knowledge and that correction(s) numbered _____ to _____ were made by me or at my request. Furthermore, I am aware that if I am determined to have knowingly made a frivolous application for asylum I will be permanently ineligible for any benefits under the Immigration and Nationality Act, and that I may not avoid a frivolous finding simply because someone advised me to provide false information in my asylum application.

Signed and sworn to before me by the above named applicant on:

_____
Signature of Applicant

_____
Date *(mm/dd/yyyy)*

_____
Write Your Name in Your Native Alphabet

_____
Signature of Immigration Judge

Addendum

Form: I-589 (Page 1)

Additional Entry History:

Date Arrived: 03/08/2013, Place: Los Angeles, CA, Status: B-2

DECLARATION OF ███████████

I, ███████████ have knowledge of the following facts, and if called to testify thereon I could and would competently testify thereto. I hereby declare as follows:

I was born on March 31, 1971 in Nassau, Bahamas.

I was raised by my mother and grandmother. My father was around but he never raised me. All three have now passed away.

I graduated high school in the Bahamas and have a Bachelor in Science in Economics and Finance from the College of the Bahamas. Prior to coming to the United States, I was working for the College of the Bahamas in an administrative/clerical position. I worked there for the College of the Bahamas for over 15 years.

Growing up in the Bahamas was extremely difficult for me. I knew I was "different" from the rest of the boys at a very young age. In elementary school, I was routinely bullied and teased, called a "sissy," for being feminine and playing with girls.

I was also in several fights as a young boy, one in the 4th grade, where I was punched in the stomach and fractured a rib. I was briefly hospitalized and missed several days of school as a result.

This discrimination and harassment continued into middle school, where even teachers called me derogatory names.

As a young boy I often did not report these incidents as I was made to believe that I was doing something "wrong." Even when I did report things to the administration, I was told to "toughen up" or "act like a man."

As a result, I never really "came out" and announced my homosexuality, not even to my mother. It was clear she knew but we never had an open discussion about it. Instead, I tried to stay out of people's way; living in the shadows in shame.

More recently, at my 20th high school reunion, I was verbally abused and publicly humiliated by a former classmate because of my sexuality while others stood and watched.

I faced similar discrimination and harassment at various places of work.

I have also seen other members of the LGBT community harassed and even attacked in the Bahamas.

If I am forced to return to the Bahamas, I will be forced to continue living in the shadows, living shame and in fear that I will be victimized again and again.

For these reasons, I pray that immigration approves my asylum application.

I declare under penalty of perjury under the laws of the State of California that the forgoing is true and correct. Executed in N. Hollywood, California.

Date: 24th Sept 2015

By: _____

GENERAL HOSPITAL

Certificate of Birth

This Certifies *that*

weight _____ *lbs.* _____ *oz. was born in this Hospital*

on the _____ *day of* _____

In Witness Whereof *this Certificate has been duly signed by the Happy Parents.*

_____

PARENTS

CERTIFIED COPY OF ENTRY IN REGISTER OF BIRTHS — **BAHAMAS**
THE BIRTHS AND DEATHS RE██████ ACT (CH. 176).

CHILD'S
CHRISTIAN OR
FIRST NAMES ████████████████████

SEX *Male*　|　DATE OF BIRTH　*31 March 1971*

PLACE OF BIRTH
Princess Margaret Hospital Nassau, Bahamas

MOTHER'S MAIDEN SURNAME ██████████　CHRISTIAN OR FIRST NAMES ████████████

MOTHER'S SURNAME AFTER MARRIAGE

FATHER'S SURNAME ██████████　CHRISTIAN OR FIRST NAMES ████████████

I CERTIFY THAT THE ABOVE STATED
PARTICULARS ARE TRUE TO THE BEST OF
MY KNOWLEDGE AND BELIEF.　████████████ (INFORMANT) *mother*

I AM SATISFIED AS TO THE CORRECTNESS
AND SUFFICIENCY OF THIS STATEMENT
AND REGISTER THE BIRTH THIS

| *9* | *July* | *1971* |
| DAY | MONTH | YEAR |

ASSISTANT
REGISTRAR *Philip Kemp*　REGISTRAR *R. E. Malone*

CORRECTIONS OR ADDITIONS

CERTIFIED TO BE A TRUE COPY OF AN ENTRY IN THE REGISTER OF BIRTHS.
GIVEN AT *Nassau, Bahs* THIS *9th* DAY OF *August*

99

19 ....

for M. M'lly
REGISTRAR GENERAL

PASSPORT

COMMONWEALTH
OF THE BAHAMAS

COMMONWEALTH
OF THE BAHAMAS

PASSPORT

These are to request and require in the name of the
Governor-General of the Commonwealth of the Bahamas
all those whom it may concern to allow the bearer
to pass freely without let or hindrance and to
afford him or her every assistance and protection
of which he or she may stand in need

No. of Passport █████████████

National Status
Citizen of the Commonwealth of The Bahamas

This Passport contains 32 pages

I

The Commonwealth of The Bahamas

Passport / Passeport

Type / Type
PR

Country Code / Code du pays
BHS

HIGGS

BAHAMIAN

31 MAR / MARS 1971

M

NEW PROVIDENCE

16 JAN / JAN 2013

15 JAN / JAN 2023

NEW PROVIDENCE

ER0126721°9BHS71033I3M2301158117817I8<<<<<<
<<<<<<<<<<<<<<<<<<<44

3

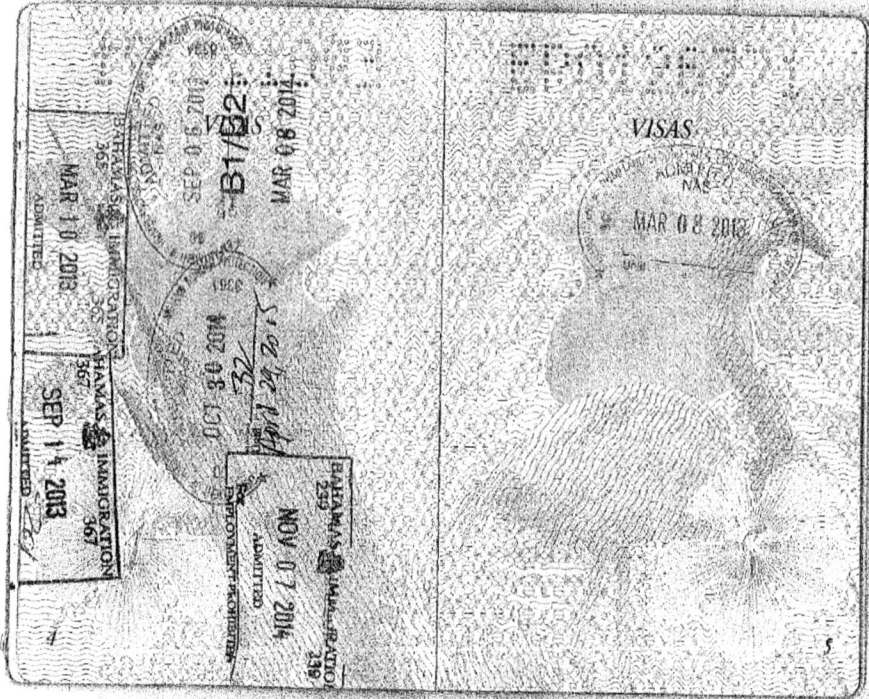

VISAS

VISAS

BAHAMAS IMMIGRATION
367
MAR 10 2013
ADMITTED

BAHAMAS IMMIGRATION
367
SEP 14 2013
ADMITTED

B1/B2

MAR 08 2014

SEP 15 2011

MAR 08 2012
NAS

NOV 07 2014
BAHAMAS IMMIGRATION
239
ADMITTED

VISAS

VISA

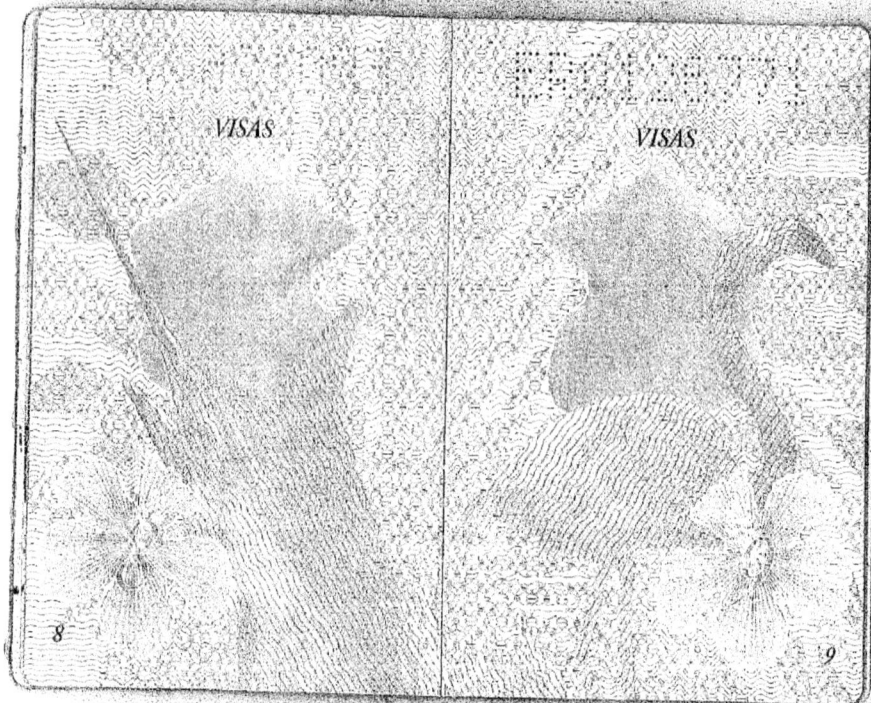

VISAS

VISAS

8

9

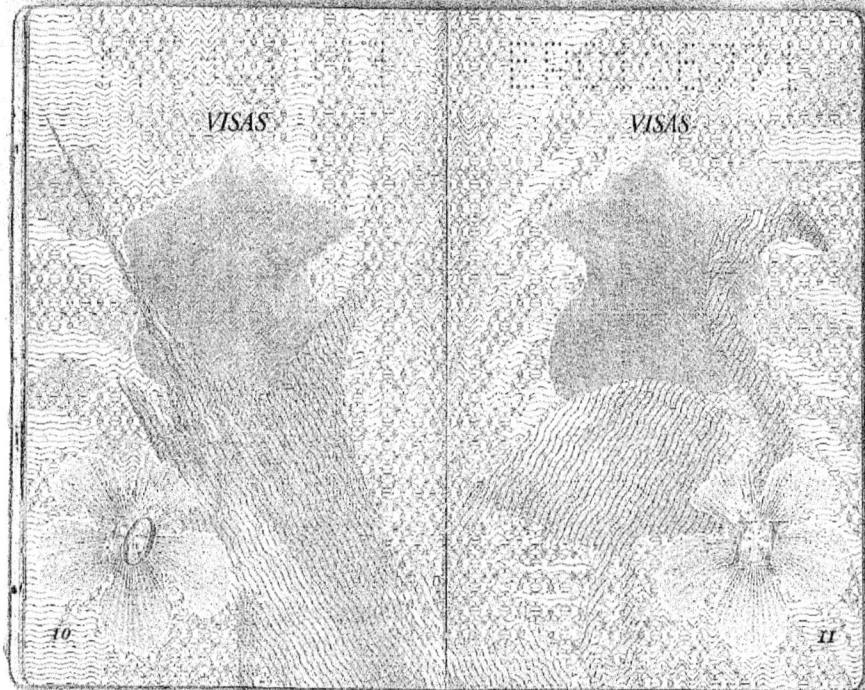

VISAS

VISAS

10

11

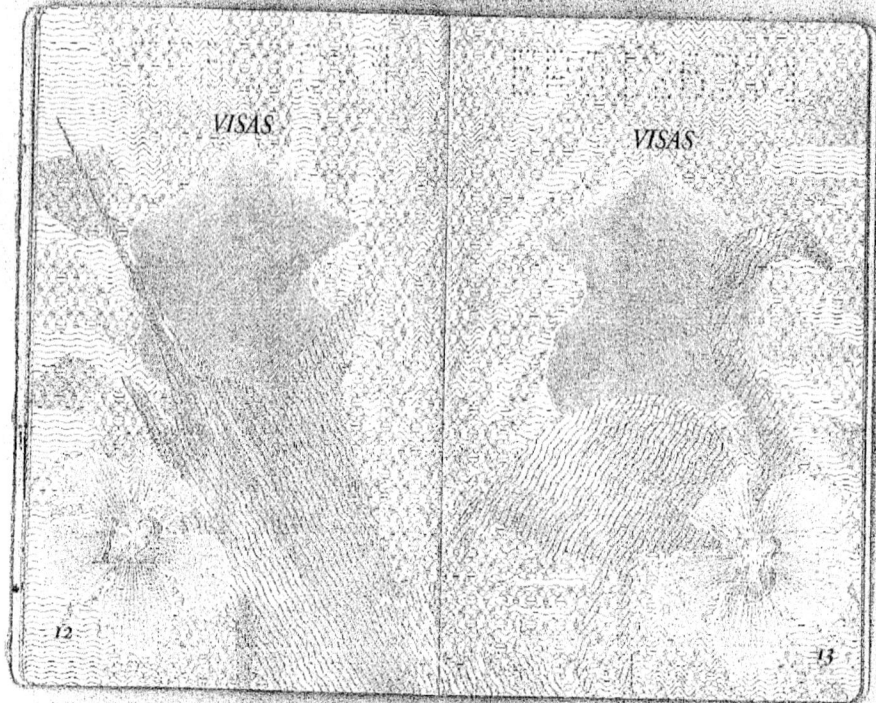

VISAS

VISAS

14

15

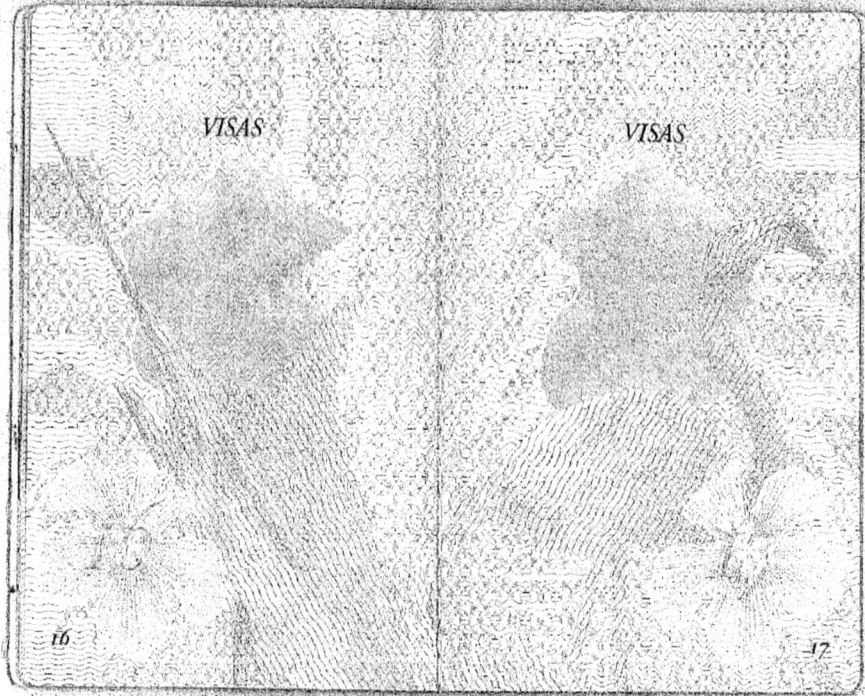

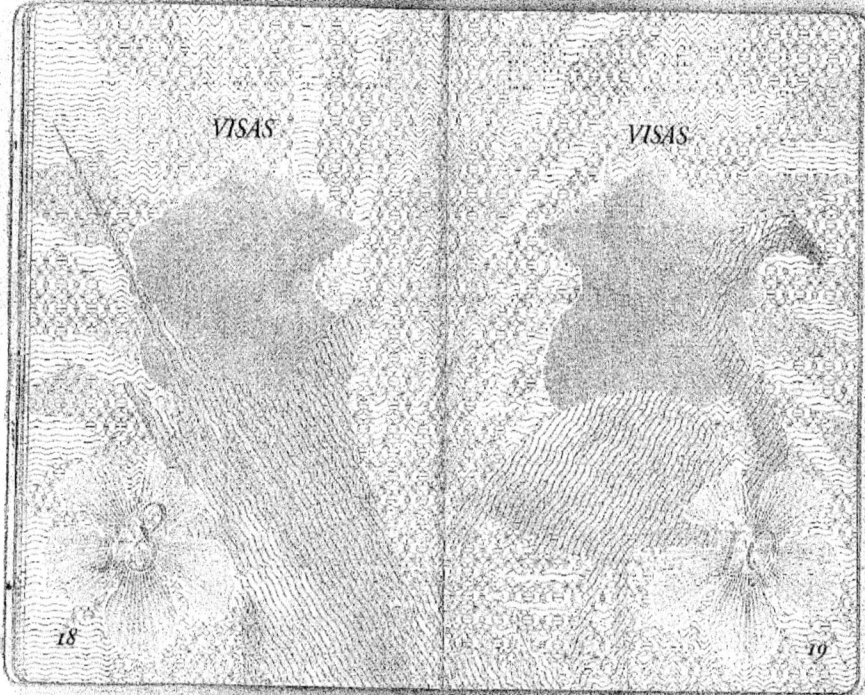

VISAS

VISAS

18

19

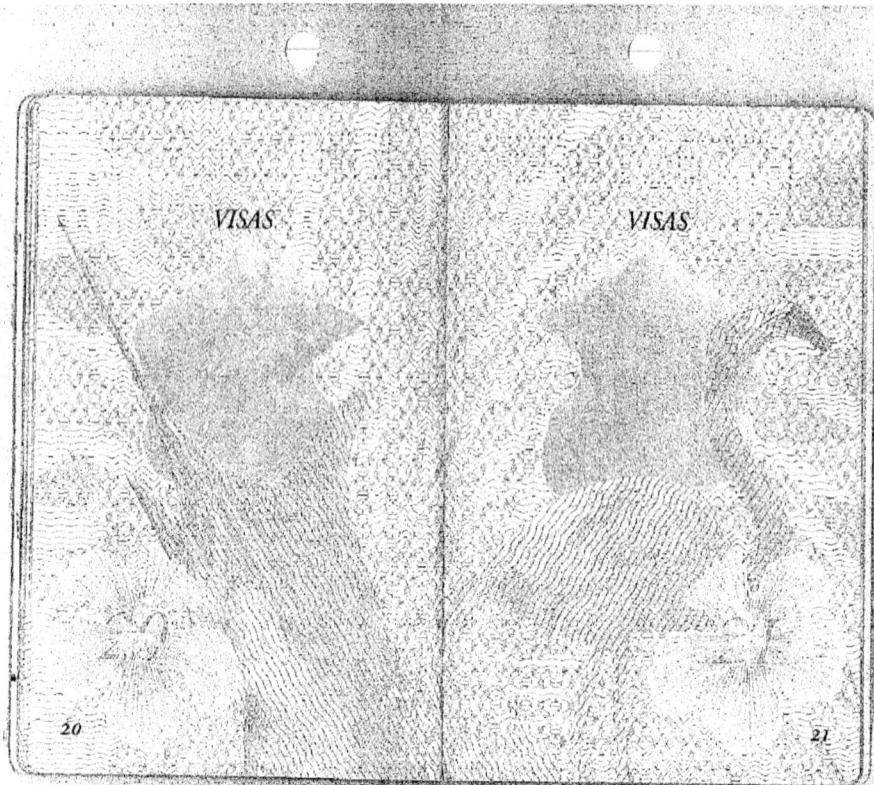

VISAS VISAS

20 21

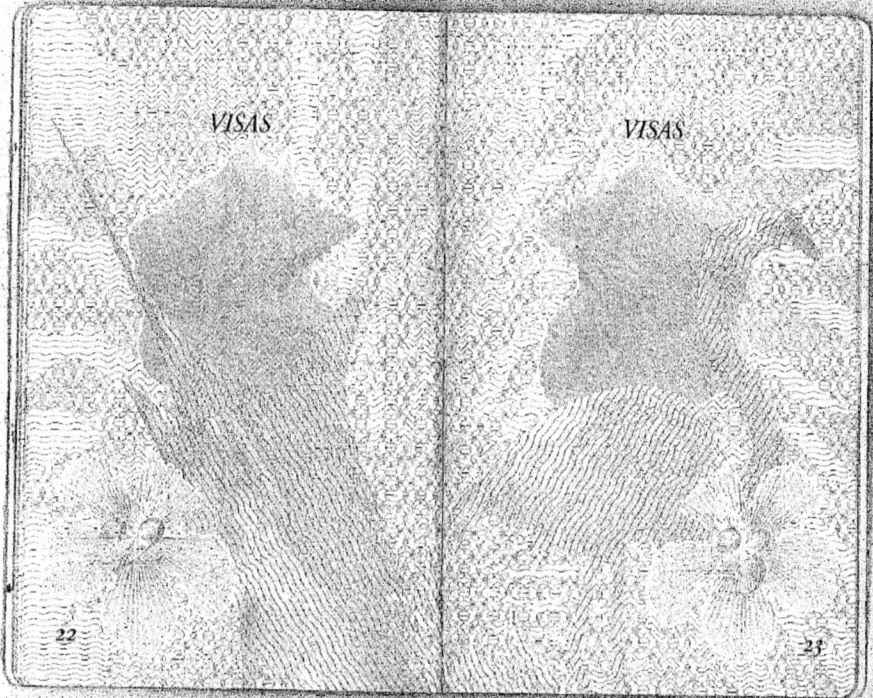

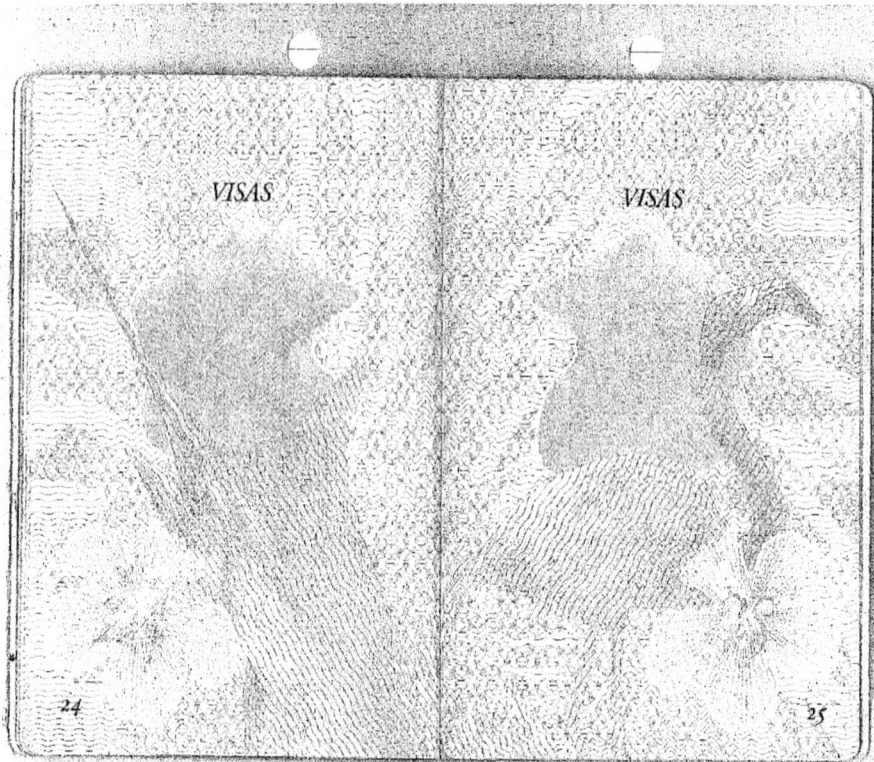

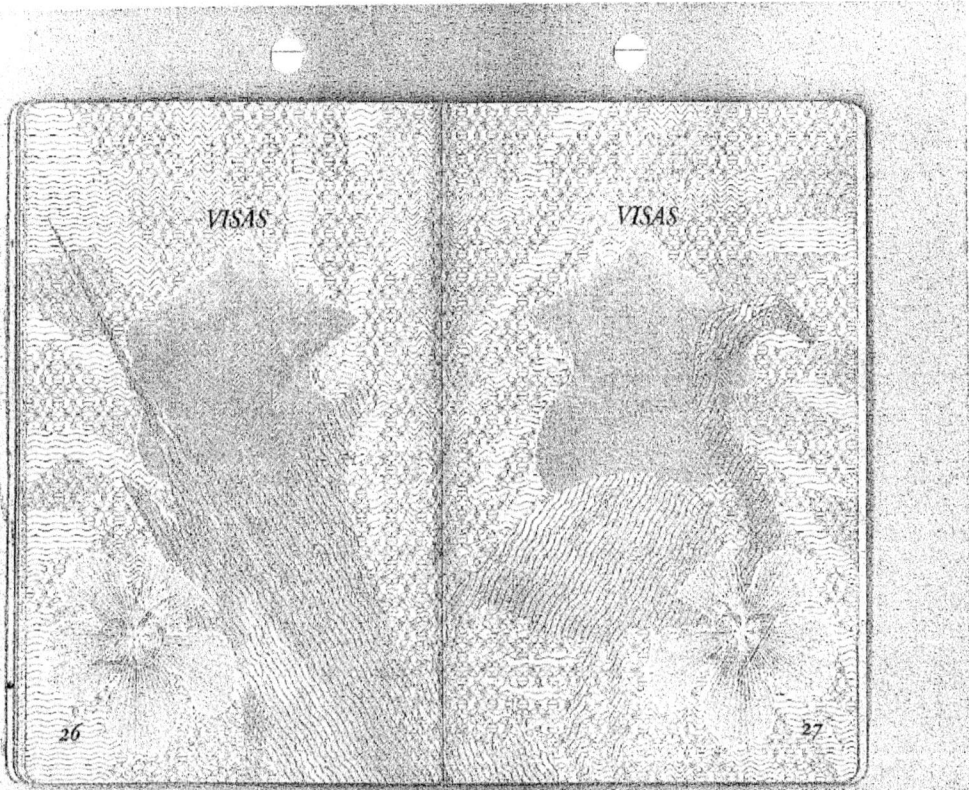

VISAS

VISAS

BAHAMAS CUSTOMS
MAR 10 2013
LPIA
EXEMPTION
09

BAHAMAS CUSTOMS
SEP 14 2013
EXEMPTION
L.P.I. AIRPORT

28

29

BANK / CURRENCY NOTATIONS

BANK / CURRENCY NOTATIONS

The holder should insert below particulars of two relatives or friends
who may be contacted in the event of accident or emergency.

Name: Name:

Address: Address:

Telephone: Telephone:

30   31

NOTES

Bahamian Passports are issued and granted by the Competent Authorities in the Commonwealth of The Bahamas and by Bahamian Diplomatic and Consular Offices in foreign countries.

Passports are available for ten years. If at any time the passport contains no further space for VISAS, a new passport must be obtained.

The possession of a passport does not exempt the holder from compliance with any immigration regulations in force in any territory or from the necessity of obtaining a visa or permit where required.

Children and wives will require separate passports.

Registration Overseas

Bahamian citizens who are resident abroad should at the earliest opportunity inform there nearest and advise at the nearest Diplomatic Mission or Consulate of the Commonwealth of The Bahamas or authorised representative. Failure to do so may, in emergency, result in difficulty or delay in according them assistance and protection. Changes of address or departure from the country should also be notified to the Mission or Consulate.

Dual Nationality

Citizens of the Commonwealth of The Bahamas who are also nationals of another country cannot avail themselves of the protection of the representatives of The Bahamas against the authorities of that country and are not, except by reason of possessing Bahamian Citizenship, freed any obligations (such as military service) to which they may be liable under the law of that country.

Caution

This Passport remains the property of the Government of the Commonwealth of The Bahamas and may be withdrawn at any time. It is a valuable document and should not be altered in any way or allowed to pass into the possession of an unauthorised person. If lost or destroyed, the fact and circumstance should be immediately reported to the Passport Office, Nassau, or the nearest Bahamian Mission or Consulate or authorised Representative abroad and to the local Police. New Passports can be issued in such cases after exhaustive enquiries have been made.

32

OMB No. 1651-0111
Expiration Date: 08/31/2015

Most Recent I-94

Admission (I-94) Record Number: ▓▓▓▓▓▓▓▓

Most Recent Date of Entry: 2015 July 01

Class of Admission: B2

Admit Until Date: 12/31/2015

Details provided on the I-94 Information form:

Last/Surname: ▓▓▓▓

First (Given) Name: ▓▓▓▓

Birth Date: ▓▓▓▓

Passport Number: ▓▓▓▓

Country of Issuance: ▓▓▓▓

[Get Travel History]

▶ Effective April 26, 2013, DHS began automating the admission process. An alien lawfully admitted or paroled into the U.S. is no longer required to be in possession of a preprinted Form I-94. A record of admission printed from the CBP website constitutes a lawful record of admission. See 8 CFR § 1.4(d).

▶ If an employer, local, state or federal agency requests admission information, present your admission (I-94) number along with any additional required documents requested by that employer or agency.

▶ Note: For security reasons, we recommend that you close your browser after you have finished retrieving your I-94 number.

For inquiries or questions regarding your I-94, please click here.

Accessibility | Privacy Policy

Judge: Killing was justified to avoid a homosexual act | Bahamas Local News

www.bahamaslocal.com/newsitem/2159/Judge_Killing_was_justified_to_avoid_a_homosexual_act.html

June 11, 2010

The Court of Appeal ruled that the court made the right decision when it sentenced Latherio Jones to three years probation for the 2004 killing of Trevor Wilson after Wilson made sexual advances towards him.

Dame Joan Sawyer, President of the Court of Appeal, said the sentence should remain because the convict had already spent almost five years awaiting trial in prison, was 18 years old at the time of the shooting and had been "provoked" to commit the violent act by his victim's sexual advance.

Dame Joan said the senior judges were not "minded to accept" the Attorney General's Office's submissions in favor of the appeal against the sentence in part because there was "no dispute by the Crown that there was a homosexual advance to (Jones) shortly before he shot (Wilson) and that it was not the only such advance."

"It was pointed out to (attorneys representing the Attorney General's Office) that had (Jones) killed (Wilson) immediately, that would be a case of self defense, because one is entitled to use whatever force is necessary to prevent one's self being the victim of a homosexual act," stated the appeal court President.

She explained that the court agreed with the trial judge's finding that "a further three years of supervision by the authorities would be of benefit to (Jones)" as opposed to a more severe sentence.

"We see nothing wrong in principle with the approach of the learned judge," she added, referring to the sentence applied by the trial judge in the case.

The dismissal of the Attorney General's appeal against the sentence given to Jones came as a surprise to some in the legal community. One criminal lawyer pointed out that manslaughter is an offence in The Bahamas which has been known to carry a sentence of between 10 and 35 years incarceration.

Nevertheless the relatively lenient stance taken by the court is reminiscent of that in the case of Frederick Green-Neely, a Bahamian man who was acquitted in 2008 of the 2005 stabbing death of Dale Williams.

Green-Neely, 25, admitted to the killing of Williams, who was allegedly gay and known to be HIV-positive, after Williams "grabbed his genitals" and told him he had a crush on him.

Click here to download the complete ruling from the Court of Appeal

Click here to read this and other judgments from the Court of Appeal website

Click here to read more in The Tribune

News date : 06/11/2010   Category : Tribune Stories

The Tribune

- Login or Sign up

Upvote 0

'I Have Been Discriminated Against For My Sexuality'

As of Wednesday, June 12, 2013

- Sign in to favorite this
- Discuss 28 comments, Blog about
- Share this Email, Facebook, Twitter

Erin Greene

By SANCHESKA BROWN

Tribune Staff Reporter

sbrown@tribunemedia.net

REFUTING the government's claim that there is no discrimination due to sexual orientation in the Bahamas, human rights activist Erin Greene complained that the records don't exist because police refuse to take complaints from the gay community.

She was responding to Attorney General Allyson Maynard-Gibson, who recommended that the

Constitutional prohibition against discrimination should be amended to exclude discrimination on the basis of sexual orientation, as there are no reports of this on record, and the country has "far more pressing matters" to deal with.

But Ms Greene said: "I am a victim of both crime and discrimination. I am a victim of stalking, for more than four years. I am unable to convince the Royal Bahamas Police Force that it is their duty to fully investigate these matters.

"I have reported both the crimes and the instances of discrimination to the RBPF, to the Commissioner of

Police and directly and to the Prime Minister.

"This matter is not only unresolved but the RBPF have indicated that they have no intention of continuing the investigation."

She said her experience is shared by several members of the gay community who feel they were attacked, victimised or discriminated against because of their sexual orientation.

"We have been unable to convince the Royal Bahamas Police Force that it is their duty to record this information (on request of the victim) when processing a crime.

"In the absence of an official mechanism (ie Human Rights Council) to record crimes and discrimination against the LGBT community, the LGBT community is unable to report acts of violence against them, or instances of discrimination."

Mrs Greene said Mrs Maynard-Gibson's comments indicate that she is not very well informed about the state of crime and violence in the country and out of touch with the developments in her profession, both locally and internationally.

She also refuted claims that gay marriage is illegal in the Bahamas.

Ms Greene said: "The fact that our government does not have the capacity to record instances of crime, violence and discrimination against the LGBT community does not mean that members of the LGBT community have not attempted to have these instances recorded by official mechanisms.

"The fact that the state refuses to issue marriage licences to same-sex couples does not mean that gay marriage is illegal in the Commonwealth of the Bahamas, as there are no provisions in law that prevent a church or minister of religion from conducting a same sex marriage ceremony."

Ms Green said the LGBT community pledges to support the Attorney General in her work, but encouraged Mrs Maynard-Gibson to use her resources to protect the rights of all Bahamians – not just some.

More like this story

- Petition calls for end to discrimination
- Mitchell: I am criticised because of my support for gay rights
- Report highlights gay man's murder
- Call for education campaign on LGBT issues
- Mitchell and gay rights

Comments

henny 2 years, 3 months ago

What do you have to say now AG Maynard Gibson??? No excuses please.

| Upvote | 1

Bahamas: Vacation   News   Real Estate   Directory   Business   Community

Current Bahamas News

Bahamas News - Home

Bahamas Information

Bahamas Island Guides
Bahamas Weather
Bahamas Map
Bahamas Vacation & Travel
Bahamas Directory
Bahamas Real Estate
Bahamas Q&A
Bahamas Classifieds
Bahamas Events Calendar

Bahamas-Travel.info

Plan your Bahamas vacation. Many pages of free travel resources available on Bahamas-Travel.info, including information on Atlantis Bahamas.

Bahamas Top Stories

2004-07-17 11:57:04

Gay Cruise Passengers Met With Angry Protest in Bahamas

Gay and lesbian cruise ship passengers met more than 100 protesters holding signs and leading anti-gay chants as they stepped off their chartered ship Friday in the Bahamas.

The protesters, led by Christian pastors, gathered in a square in front of the cruise terminal and chanted: "Gay ways are not God's ways!" As a trickle of passengers stepped out, protesters held signs reading: If You're Openly Gay, Stay Away and We Will Not Bow to the Gay Agenda!

Former talk show host Rosie O'Donnell, a cruise promoter, was aboard the Norwegian Dawn but wasn't among those who disembarked.

Gregg Kominsky, a founder of cruise organizer R Family Vacations, said the passengers - 1,150 adults and 450 children - had come to have fun and that on previous trips he found most Bahamians friendly and welcoming.

"We are not really here to make a statement," he said.

Kominsky said he was disappointed by the protest but people have a right to their opinions.

As the first passengers stepped out, shouting protesters pressed to within a metre of them. Police stepped in to move demonstrators back.

"We will never accept your lifestyle," said Pastor William Hanchell, who stood on a stage and spoke.

"We don't care how much money they bring. The Bahamas is off-limits," said another, Pastor Vaughan Miller.

Organizers said the demonstration was intended to be peaceful and there were no arrests.

Homosexuals have faced icy receptions in the Caribbean before. A number of islands have laws banning homosexual sex and many countries remain socially conservative.

In 1998, a protest was held in the Bahamas when a ship arrived with lesbian passengers. That same year, the Cayman Islands turned away a gay cruise following protests.

Friday's demonstration was held by a group calling itself Save the Bahamas, which led an earlier anti-cruise rally with several hundred people Sunday.

The U.S. Embassy issued a statement Thursday saying the

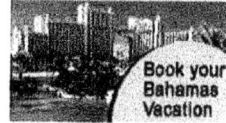

mostly American passengers deserved the right to visit in peace.

While scores of passengers disembarked, many stayed on the ship.

O'Donnell's partner, Kelli O'Donnell, got off and greeted members of the Bahamas' Rainbow Alliance, a gay and lesbian group. She helped found R Family Vacations, which promoted the seven-day cruise that began in New York City on Sunday and also made stops in Florida.

Passengers Stacey and Jessie Paris, of New Jersey, said they didn't feel welcome on their first trip to the Bahamas.

"It's very, very sad," Stacey Paris said.

She came with her biological daughter, 15-month-old Torin, and adopted son, Zion, four.

When reporters asked how they felt about the protest, Stacey turned to Zion, who was wearing a T-shirt that read Let My Parents Marry, and asked: "What do we call people like that?"

He replied: "Narrow-minded," and hugged Paris.

When the couple tried to walk through the protest, pushing a stroller, protesters told them to avoid the area and they did.

After a five-hour stop, the ship left for New York.

Source: Canadian Press

Next:

- Nine-Year-Old Was Murdered – 2004-07-17 11:57:04
- Government Pledge To Small Hotel Owners – 2004-07-17 11:57:04
- Pirate Cab Drivers Destroying Bahamas Vacations – 2004-07-17 11:57:04
- Bahamas Turns Down 35 U.S. Extradition Requests – 2004-07-17 11:57:04
- Strike threat against Atlantis – 2004-07-17 11:57:04

Previous:

- Intolerance on Display as Bahamians Protest Gay Cruise – 2004-07-17 11:57:04
- Stubbs Loses Appeal – 2004-07-17 11:57:04
- BCC Responds To Statement On Gay Cruise Protests – 2004-07-17 11:57:04
- Anti-Gay Rally Warns The Prime Minister – 2004-07-17 11:57:04
- Celebrating Bahamian Independence – 2004-07-17 11:57:04

The Bahamas Network

BAHAMASB2B (HTTP://WWW.BAHAMASB2B.COM/)   BLOG (HTTP://WWW.BAHAMASB2B.COM/BLOG/)
BUSINESS (HTTP://WWW.BAHAMASB2B.COM/BUSINESS.HTML)   CALENDAR (HTTP://WWW.BAHAMASB2B.COM/CALENDAR/)
DIRECTORY (HTTP://WWW.BAHAMASB2B.COM/DIRECTORY/)   REAL ESTATE (HTTP://WWW.BAHAMASB2B.COM/REAL-ESTATE.HTML)
SOCIETY (HTTP://WWW.BAHAMASB2B.COM/BAHAMAS.HTML)   TRAVEL (HTTP://WWW.BAHAMASB2B.COM/TRAVEL.HTML)

05:04:07 pm
Tuesday 22nd, September 2015

2008-06-20 10:36:01

Keith Bell's Deafening Silence

By John Marquis

The Tribune

Keith Bell's outburst against the judicial system, remarkable though it was, was more astounding for what he didn't say. When asked whether political pressure had ever been applied on police intelligence investigators, he declined to answer.

The silence which followed was a more eloquent condemnation of the Bahamas political and legal fraternity - the real culprits behind the nation's decline into chaos - than a million words could ever have achieved.

Mr Bell's damning silence in response to a penetrating question put to him by College of the Bahamas lecturer Michael Stevenson at a public forum last week said everything we need to know about the country's current woes.

It said very powerfully that not only had some politicians put pressure on the police, and thus hampered their ability to do their job, they had also used the kind of intimidatory tactics that had plunged even a man of Mr Bell's intelligence into frightened silence.

Mr Bell's outspoken assessment of the country's crime crisis was welcome because it helped to put flesh on bones already uncovered by several local justice campaigners, including The Tribune itself. But his refusal to answer Mr Stevenson's question publicly confirmed what I among others already knew - that political interference in the law enforcement and judicial process has done much to inflict virtually irreparable damage to law and order in this country.

The case of Barrie Best was not, of course, the first high-profile murder to fall foul of selective justice and political interference. That dubious honour fell to the Sir Harry Oakes case of 1943, when powerful local interests - namely, the ruling white oligarchy of the day - conspired to corrupt justice to such an extent that an innocent man was almost sent to the gallows.

Best, however, was in at the beginning of the modern era of selective justice. And his brutal murder in 1979 set the pattern for much of what is happening today.

When Best was savaged to death, presumably by a gay lover, though that was never proved, nearly three decades ago police were told bluntly that the investigation must not be allowed to run its course, The reason: the flamboyant music teacher was involved in a gay sex, ring which included several prominent and influential people.

Arrest of his killer would have resulted in potentially embarrassing disclosures from the witness-box. Names would have been called, reputations would have been ruined, and society itself would have been rocked to its base.

This information has reached me from good sources and, in the light of everything that has happened since, is almost certain to be true.

There is no doubt that many senior figures in Nassau - from politics, business, the law, the church, and even law enforcement agencies - are heavily engaged in covert homosexual activity which is having a direct impact on law and order.

Best's killer, along with the killer or killers of handbag designer Harl Taylor, academic Dr Thaddeus McDonald, AIDS activist Wellington Adderley and Jamaican waiter Marvin Wilson, presumably continues to walk around Nassau to this day, immune to due process because of his gay connections, though two prominent suspects are already dead.

Lump him in with the suspected killer of nightclub manager Joy Cartwright, the suspected killer of Sgt Kevin Williams, and the many other suspected killers with gay or political connections who are still on the loose and an alarming picture begins to emerge.

This is especially so when you count in suspected murderers out on bail because of official inability or unwillingness to process them and an unfortunate precedent set by the courts some years ago when a wealthy, white Bahamian was allowed bail in a murder case. Nassau is crawling with killers.

Little wonder, then, that violent crime is soaring to unacceptable new levels, and that the city's lowlife is beginning to see itself as untouchable. Mr Bell compounded that unpalatable reality by revealing that police have stopped shipments of heavy weaponry, including grenades and explosives, coming into the country, presumably for use by local drug gangs.

The villains are becoming so cocky that they are preparing for war on their own terms, with the kind of hardware that is familiar on the streets of Gaza, Mogadishu or Baghdad, but has not until recent years been a feature of Nassau life - or death.

In fact, Trinidad and Jamaica, countries laid low by crime, are now being cited as the kind of societies the Bahamas is destined to become within a few-years if nothing is done to arrest the current decline.

That is a terrifying thought because, unlike them, the Bahamas has only one industry to speak of - the notoriously fragile tourism business, which will disappear literally overnight if a full-scale gunfight ever breaks out in Bay Street. It requires only one AK-47, one rocketlauncher or one hand-grenade to be used in the wrong place, and the Bahamas can say goodbye to its primary breadwinner. As Mr Bell rightly pointed out, the talking must stop. Action is overdue.

The belief that the entire legal system is at breaking point is reaffirmed more or less continually by the lone voices in Nassau society that report the ghastly truth from street level.

The names Greg and Tanya Cash, Clever Duncombe, Felix Bethel, Harald Fuhrmann and Rodney Moncur are all too familiar to readers of the Bahamian press as justice campaigners who are willing to go on the record with their complaints.

But they actually represent a much wider public, people who are less bold but no less disgruntled in their battles with the courts and the legal system in general. In their own way, the campaigners are the Bahamas' counterparts of the pressure groups you find in first world societies, and are therefore crucial to the process. Constantly, insistently, ordinary Bahamians urge them to continue the fight on their behalf.

Among Mr Bell's disclosures was that 11,000 criminal cases are caught up in the judicial backlog, along with 48,000 traffic offences. A grand total of 100,000 cases await resolution.

Among them are some of particular interest to those who keep a close watch on the courts, and wonder whether the judicial process will be thwarted by outside interference.

These observers are especially keen to know when the retrial will occur of the man accused of murdering the aforementioned Joy Cartwright. At the moment, he is out on bail.

Ms Cartwright died in a hail of bullets inside her Nassau apartment around 12 years ago. A man was tried and convicted of her murder, sentenced to death, but was then freed on appeal to await a retrial.

The case is of interest because of Ms Cartwright's high-level political connections. She was known to have been "emotionally involved" with at least one senior politician and the son of a prominent legal family, among others.

Ms Cartwright, an ambitious woman who liked wealthy men who could gratify her materialistic instincts, was described to me as "into jewellery and big cars" with a voracious appetite for money.

That appetite allegedly led to her demise, because she was suspected - according to accusations in a US court - of misappropriating nearly two million dollars belonging to the Boston mafia. Nine bullets were allegedly fired into her upper body as she entered her apartment after returning from work.

Another case of concern involves several Defence Force marines accused of a brutal beating incident in Inagua. There was a suggestion at the time that a political cover-up was underway. The case is now being watched closely by those who are anxious to see it reach court.

A case of arms smuggling, when ammunition was found wrapped in baby clothes being shipped into Nassau, is another under close scrutiny, along with a police shooting in Bimini, and a sexual assault case involving minors in Freeport. A source said: "These cases are being tracked to ensure they don't disappear. If they don't come up for hearing soon, we shall be asking some awkward questions."

Mr Bell is not alone among ex-policemen in expressing concern about the massive case backlog and the upsurge in violent crime.

Former assistant police commissioner Paul Thompson is appalled at long court delays, some stretching to five years or more, and the effect they are having on police morale.

Not only have these delays led to murder suspects being freed on bail, because the courts did not feel justified in holding them in custody any longer, they have also been weakened by loss of witnesses, who die or disappear while waiting to give evidence.

Mr Thompson is now advocating importation of foreign judges on short fixed-term contracts who can relieve existing judges of the case backlog. "I just can't understand why it takes so long to get these cases before the courts," he said.

Hardline foreign judges who would take no nonsense from local attorneys who use unwarranted adjournments to thwart the legal process are desperately needed to help the Bahamas regain control, he said.

"This deterioration in the judicial system began about 30 years ago," he said, "that's when the backlog began to build up. Now it's reached a point where it is unacceptable."

As the debate over unresolved crimes rages on, the gay murder saga continues to cause both disquiet and disenchantment.

Echoes of Barrie Best and Sgt Williams are inevitable as detectives fail to produce a culprit or culprits in the Taylor, McDonald, Adderley and Wilson murders. Sgt Williams, an acknowledged homosexual, was shot dead at his Bernard Road home seven years ago. His killer is widely thought to have been a police colleague. An arrest is considered unlikely.

Unless someone is exerting undue pressure on the current inquiry, it is hard to understand why police are making such hard work of it on an island only 21 miles by seven with a known gay scene and an extensive bi-sexual underground fraternity.

Though investigators are reluctant to link the four murders, there are several similarities which point to such a conclusion.

Firstly, all the victims were killed in their own homes by people who, it seems, were known to them.

All died in extremely bloody circumstances, with McDonald pummelled by a clothing iron to the point where his features were no longer recognisable, Taylor knifed repeatedly in his upper body, Adderley slashed across his throat in a virtual beheading, and Wilson run through with a dagger from his own ornamental arms collection.

Each scene, it appears, was awash with blood, with powerful forensic evidence readily available, including palm prints and footprints in at least two of the incidents.

These killings bore all the, hallmarks of homosexual rage, possibly the result of emotions running high over relationships or liaisons gone wrong, or revenge resulting from disease transmission.

For what it's worth, a source close to Nassau's gay community told me last week that these were the two likeliest explanations for all four killings, with the "spurned lover" scenario being the preferred option.

"I think these killings were definitely committed by a gay or gays," he said, claiming that homosexuals were particularly dangerous when sexual liaisons went wrong.

"You don't ever want to get beaten by a sissy," he said, "They don't ever accept the word 'No'. If they are in love with you, they will kill you."

All four murders suggested vicious spats; probably spontaneous rather than calculated, with no signs of forced entry at any of the premises involved.

In each case, the killer or killers must have been blood-spattered because of the sheer quantity of gore found at the scene. It is hard to believe, therefore, that no-one in Nassau knows who the culprit or culprits are, which suggests they are being protected.

"It's likely this is the work of a serial killer," the source told INSIGHT, "He was probably picked up for sex in each case, then turned against the victim for whatever reason."

In the Wilson murder, a condom and lubricant were reportedly found on the victim's bed, suggesting that the attack occurred during preparations for, or after, sex. "Don't rule out the possibility of a foreigner," said the source, "black guys are keen on white guys or anyone who can help them with their finances. "All gay men need to be doubly vigilant now. They need to know who they are picking up and being picked up by. They need to be careful who they let into their house or into their car."

In a notoriously promiscuous homosexual environment, this is easier said than done. Multiple partners are commonplace in gay circles, and 'rent boys' add another dimension to the problem. But there is no doubt that gays are now concerned about where the killer will strike next, and whether they will be the ones with the knife at their necks.

Inevitably, the net result of a malfunctioning judicial system is vigilante justice. Exasperated Bahamian families are being driven to revenge attacks, according to fathers' rights crusader Clever Duncombe.

His group, he says, counsels and mediates in situations where desperate men arm themselves to get even, having been victims of crime. "There would be more vigilante crime in this country if it weren't for groups like ours," he told INSIGHT.

Tanya Cash also fears an upsurge in revenge crime which, she says, is "all the talk" in the communities.

Mr Bell's strictures on the crime crisis are important because it is unusual for anyone so recently connected with the upper reaches of the police force to be so candid.

What he said surprised no-one who has been studying the subject in recent years, and certainly, came as no shock to INSIGHT readers, but his words - the products of many years in the force - carry an authority others often don't.

As the economy slows down, and jobs become scarcer, Mr Bell's gloomy assessment of Nassau's crime problems is likely to become gloomier still, with more and more youngsters seeing crime as their only career option.

"It's going to get a lot worse unless we take the bull by the horns and make some very tough decisions," said Mr Bell. But it's that studied silence that will reverberate most in the minds of those who really know what this society is all about, where the real problem lies, and why there is so little apparent will to tackle crime.

Last week, former Cabinet minister Dr Bernard Nottage at last acknowledged in parliament the role of politicians in the nation's plight. A failure to provide leadership, and an example others could follow, were at its root, he said.

"This is not the Bahamas I know and love. Something has gone terribly wrong and we in the House have to accept a large part of the blame for this sad state of affairs."

Then he said all plans for improving the economy will come to nought if nothing was done to get a handle on criminality. And he decried as "disgraceful" the extent to which national institutions like parliament and the judicial system had been allowed to sink.

What we are witnessing now, in fact, is the cumulative effect of decades of slackness in which political, religious, familial and sometimes professional affiliations have been allowed to interfere with the legal process.

It began under the UBP, accelerated rapidly under the Pindling regime, and is now so much part of the Bahamian way of life that even senior politicians themselves are unable to discern where right ends and wrong begins.

Political expediency, and a desire to protect certain sections of society, have been allowed to intrude all too often in criminal investigations. Barrie Best was a case in point, and so was the failure to prosecute certain figures involved in the 1984 Commission of Inquiry into drug-trafficking.

More blatant still was the failure - for purely political reasons - to take the right course in the Joy Cartwright murder inquiry.

In all these cases, police were left impotent, having been scuppered by political interference.

No senior politician need express surprise when confronted by the dire circumstances now facing the Bahamas. Many of them, to their eternal shame have been direct contributors to the problem. The law has been the plaything of the privileged. Now it's time to count the cost.

When Mr Stevenson asked the question about political interference, Mr Bell indicated that he would talk to him privately after the meeting. We were not privy to that conversa- tion, but it takes little by way of genius to guess what might have been said.

Dr Nottage claimed "a very dangerous state of affairs" would result if politicians failed to command the respect of the people. What he didn't say was that such a situation is already at hand, and that cynicism and mistrust are running so deep that do-it-yourself justice is already a reality.

By JOHN MARQUIS, Managing Editor
The Tribune
Nassau, Bahamas
June 16, 2008
Read More (1)

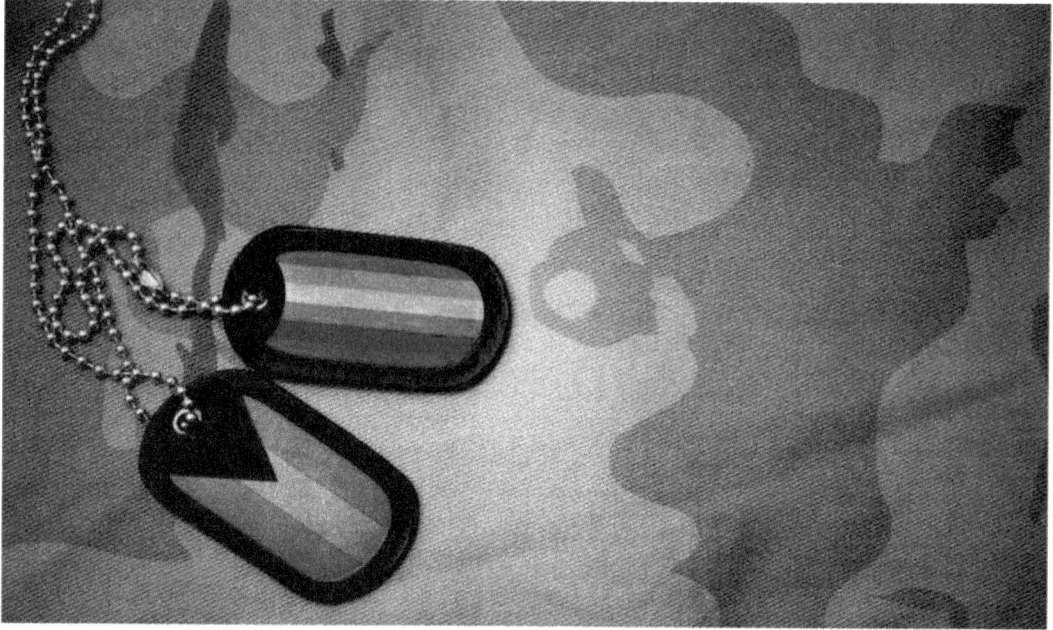

Erin Greene - "History of Rainbow Alliance Bahamas" – Activist Report

History of Rainbow Alliance in The Bahamas (RAB)

Erin Greene - Activist Report

1. How and why did Rainbow Alliance get started in Nassau? What local/national/global political struggles gave rise to Rainbow Alliance?

The Rainbow Alliance of the Bahamas (RAB) was a support and advocacy group. The Rainbow Alliance of the Bahamas was formed in 2003 to advocate on behalf of the LGBT community. RAB was formed as a vehicle to respond to these comments: "if Parliament legalizes gay marriage, I will become the next Guy Fawkes..." made by the then President of the Bahamas Christian Council, Bishop Samuel Greene at the National Independence Church Service in July 2003. At the time, Bishop Greene also sat on the Constitutional Reform Committee that was required to include the issue of sexual orientation and gender discrimination in its "Options for Change."

The Rainbow Alliance of the Bahamas was formed by members of the Pride Committee, Bahamians Gays and Lesbians Against Discrimination (BGLAD), members of the former group Hope TEA and other individuals. At the time of Bishop Greene's statement, the Pride committee was planning the 3rd Annual Pride Celebrations and decided to postpone the event to focus on the statement and the upcoming constitutional reform exercise.

2. What were the successes and challenges of organizing through Rainbow Alliance?

When formed RAB consisted of a small core group of members, with the intention of adding new members at various levels. Soon after formation, the core group realized that formal membership would be difficult to attract due to the stigma and fear of discrimination and visibility experienced by the LGBT community. After several years of work, it was believed by many Bahamians that RAB had a membership in the thousands. This perception afforded a layer of protection for RAB spokespersons and the LGBT community that continues to this day. (I believe this perception that RAB had thousands of members made individuals think twice before discriminating against members of the community). Unlike many regional LGBT organizations, the Rainbow Alliance had three spokespersons that identified as homosexuals, did not use pseudonyms and made television and radio appearances. This allowed the organization to establish trust with Bahamians at large and the LGBT community in particular. Most members of the core group were already established activists who had worked with other LGBT groups and human rights issues. The Rainbow Alliance was able to attract several heterosexual members and allies who were willing to be visible advocates for the group, including several members of the clergy.

Community visibility was always been a major concern for RAB. Organizing public and private activities was difficult as members of the LGBT community were committed to protecting their privacy at all costs even from other members of the same community. Even though RAB was able to create a community centre and office space, outside of a movie series, informal church services and one major cookout fundraiser, RAB was not able to sustain the community centre and its activities. We were unable to convince the community that the centre was a safe space, and it closed it doors after a year of operation. At this point, several core members left RAB as they had committed to developing the support elements of the organization.

RAB also experienced resistance from a number of owners of LGBT bars and clubs. The community centre was designated a drug and alcohol free space and it was perceived as an attempt to attract customers from the other establishments. In the Bahamas, an individual under the age of eighteen cannot access medical services or health and sexual health information without the consent of a parent or guardian, also homosexual sex is illegal for individuals under the age of eighteen. This prevented RAB from offering programs for LGBT youth, and prevented interaction with members of the community that wanted to volunteer, intern and be involved in the movement generally.

One of the largest challenges faced by RAB was that it was perceived of as a white upper-middle class organization comprised of privileged individuals that had a level of financial security and stability that made it possible for them to maintain a level of visibility that the average homosexual Bahamian could not. Many black working-class Bahamians felt that RAB was asking the LGBT community to face head-on challenges that the core members of the organization did not have to face because of social status and privilege. At the climax of RAB's work, it was determined that the statutory and legislative framework necessary for LGBT rights and protections were already in place[i] and the political community was prepared to represent a minority group that was willing to demand representation. Unfortunately during the time of RAB's organizing work, many in the LGBT community were not willing to assume the visibility necessary to participate in the democratic process.

3. What happened to the organization and how did this affect sexual minority organizing in the Bahamas?

The organization closed its doors in December 2008 after all but one of the core members decided to focus their energies on other human rights issues and personal endeavors. Two of the core members had just been elected to the executive board of Caribbean Forum for Lesbians All-Sexual and Gays (CFLAG) and felt that they could continue their work locally as a part of this regional body. At the time of its closing, RAB was the only LGBT advocacy group in the country. Shortly thereafter, the organization Sexual Addicts Seeking Healing (SASH Bahamas) had completed its transition to Society Against STIs and HIV/AIDS (SASH Bahamas) and became an HIV/AIDS focused action and Gay support group. Transgender and transsexual Bahamians continued to organize within Pageant houses in the absence of RAB. And recently in July 2011, a new sexual minority organization has formed: the Bahamas LGBT Equality Advocates (BLEA) is a non-profit LGBT support and advocacy organization. BLEA stands against homophobia, agitates for the removal of laws that discriminate against LGBT people, and fights stigma and discrimination on the basis of sexual orientation, gender identity and HIV status.

4. How did the HIV/AIDS pandemic affect the work of Rainbow Alliance?

The major stakeholders in the HIV/AIDS activist community whether formally or informally decided that it would be more effective strategically to not publicly align with the LGBT rights movement and RAB. RAB presumed that this strategy was aimed at not ostracizing major stakeholders and funders in HIV/AIDS work like the Christian community.

5. How did Rainbow Alliance address language in terms of same-sex relationships and gender variance? To what extent were the terms "lesbian," "transgender," "gay," and "bisexual" used for self-naming?

In its work RAB found that the LGBT community as a whole was resistant to the use of labels and language used to categorize orientation and define behavior. Many members of the community didn't even feel a need to identify as homosexual, and felt that these terms lesbian and transgender etc. were a part of being visible that they were unwilling to engage.

Even when Bahamians became comfortable with engaging the homosexual community in discourse, they were not prepared to discuss transphobia and transgender issues. RAB made a conscious decision to not focus on transphobia and transgender issues in its media work, but never shied away from the topic if raised in discussion or while addressing specific transgender issues. While RAB did not want to alienate this segment of the LGBT community, it was necessary to maintain a dialogue with a resistant and intolerant wider audience.

6. Did the spread of Western LGBT politics impact your local organizing?

It became apparent that anti-gay proponents in their statements and activities were in the majority of instances responding to events or statements made in North and South America and Europe including the United Kingdom. It is believed that Bishop Greene's infamous statements were commentary on the movement to legalize same sex marriage and civil unions in The United States. After July 2004, it was assumed by society at large, including the gay community, that the Rainbow Alliance had initiated a campaign to legalize same sex marriage in the Bahamas, like its American counterparts. However, this was not on RAB's agenda. The assumption was made because RAB organized a counter protest to the protest of Rosie O'Donnell 'Our Family' Cruise in July 2004. The local protest called their campaign "Save the Family," but they were really protesting foreigners who were thought to be flaunting a "lifestyle" (supposedly) abhorred by Bahamians, which in this case had to be endured because of our reliance on tourism. RAB's counter protest was held not to promote same sex marriage, but rather to show the international community that Bahamian sexual minorities exist and have a presence in The Bahamas.

Many Bahamians questioned the need for LGBT advocacy at all, asserting that the Bahamas is nowhere near as violent as Jamaica or Middle Eastern and certain African States. And although the Bahamas was not a target country in the "StopMurderMusic" Campaign, the Rainbow Alliance observed the disconnect between international activists and activists on the ground in Jamaica, and agreed with Jamaican activists that the resistance from Jamaicans at large and the LGBT community in particular to the campaign was more about sovereignty and post-colonial political and diasporic power dynamics and less to do with homophobia.

International LGBT activists generally disregard the importance of religion and spirituality in Caribbean states and thus alienate the majority of the local LGBT community from their work. RAB found the vast majority of homosexual Bahamians identify as Christian and do not wish to end their relationship with their religious communities, and they prioritize building healthy relationships with religious institutions and encourage dialogue with the Christian community in particular.

7. In what ways have you documented the history of Rainbow Alliance? What would you like fellow Caribbeans to know about the work of Rainbow Alliance?

The work of the Rainbow Alliance is being documented through several archiving projects, including Caribbean IRN. All of the organization's media appearances can be found in the archives of local print, television, radio and electronic media houses.

I The Sexual Offences and Domestic Violence Act 1991 (s.5B(1), which speaks specifically to sexual intercourse in a public place, ultimately decriminalized homosexual intercourse for men because it made the colonial sodomy laws null and void, but essentially criminalized homosexual intercourse for women. It is believed that the change in law was argued on the basis of a constitutional right to privacy and that the law itself was intended to monitor behaviour in public places only. Prior to the 2008 amendment to the Sexual Offences and Domestic Violence Act 1991, the age of consent for homosexual intercourse was 18, while the age of consent for heterosexual intercourse remained at 16. And a person found guilty of engaging in homosexual intercourse in a public place was liable to a term of imprisonment for life. After the 2008 amendments to the act, it is unclear what the age of consent is for homosexual intercourse as there is no clear definition of age of consent for "unnatural sex" in the amended act. Also the penalty for engaging in homosexual intercourse in a public space was reduced to a term of imprisonment for two years.

Activist Reports

Las Krudas – "Kandela" - Music Video

Erin Greene - "History of Rainbow Alliance Bahamas" – Activist Report

Sekou Charles & Colin Robinson – "Riding Boundaries" - Short Film and Poem

Lawrence Scott - "Chameleon" - Short Story

Joanne Hillhouse - "Differences" - Poem

Suriname Men United - "Public Campaign against Dancehall Artists" - Activist Report

Lawrence Graham-Brown – "10 Minutes Into The Honeymoon" - Performance Art

Vidyaratha Kissoon – "No Weapon formed against Me shall Prosper" - Activist Report

and Lesbophobia in Caribbean Culture" - Critical Essay

Rodell Warner - Visual Art, Photography

Maria Govan and Kareem Mortimer - Interview with Angelique V. Nixon - Video

"Complexities of Place" - Activist Roundtable

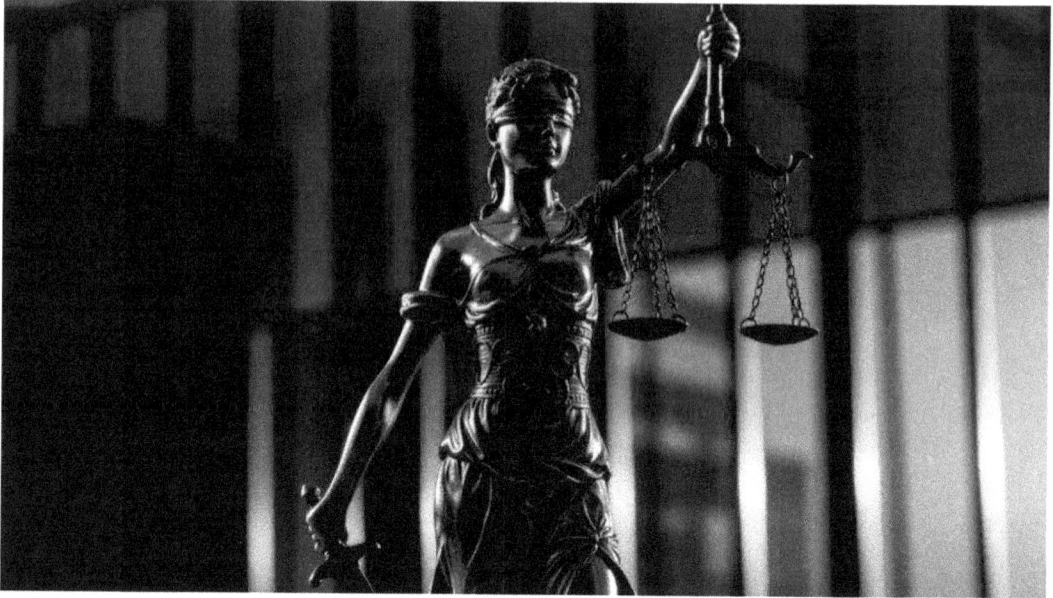

Guardian

Government against gay marriages

CHESTER ROBARDS
Guardian Staff Reporter
chester@nasguard.com

Published: Jul 08, 2011

There will be no change to the definition of marriage as being between a man and a woman under the Ingraham administration, Minister of State for Finance Zhivargo Laing said yesterday.

Laing's comments came during debate on a Maritime Marriage Bill to legalize maritime marriages in Bahamian waters.

Laing said several pieces of legislation will be consolidated to clearly define marriage as being between a man and a woman.

Laing said the Maritime Marriage Bill's purpose is two-fold: seeking to produce another source of revenue for The Bahamas and to facilitate the "dream to get married in The Bahamas" even if it is aboard a seagoing vessel.

However, the purpose of consolidating the four marriage acts currently under law is to weave the clause that ensures marriage is between a man and a woman into them collectively. The four acts of law pertaining to marriage are the Marriage Act, the Marriage of Deceased Wife's Sister Act, the Marriage of British Subjects Act and the Foreign Marriages Act.

"As a community in The Bahamas we believe that a marriage must and should be and is between a man and a woman," Laing said.

"A marriage is void if it took place between persons who were male and male or female and female. So, in this Maritime Marriage Bill we are stating this fact in the clear positive — a marriage must take place between a male and a female and we want that to be abundantly clear that, that is so and that is keeping with our community standard."

After the government recently backed a United Nations resolution in support of rights for gay, lesbian, bi-sexual and transgender (GLBT) people, the Bahamas Christian Council (BCC) condemned it as a possible "hidden agenda" which it feared could eventually lead to gay marriage.

The position of the BCC was that it supports the protection of everyone from all forms of discrimination, which the resolution offered.

However, it warned that The Bahamas government's support of the UN resolution could open a spigot that allows for all rights afforded heterosexuals to be offered to GLBT people, including marriage.

The BCC insisted in its release that the institution of marriage should only be consecrated between a man and a woman.

Laing said the government considered the commercial and economic interests of recognizing marriages at sea, while remembering that the Christian convictions and the societal status quo with regard to marriage in this country had to be upheld — even at sea.

"In taking this decision we didn't do so lightly," Laing said.

"We wanted very deliberately to balance the commercial interest and advancement that could be afforded us by doing this, with our recognition that marriage, in the context of our Christian convictions broadly in this society, must be sanctified in a certain way and defined in a certain way.

"We wanted there to be no mistakes, notwithstanding the developing and evolving realities in the world in which we live, that in this country there is a standard, there is a set of communal convictions that govern our definition of marriage and the extent to which we sanctify it in this society."

This content has been locked. You can no longer post any comment.

SPORTS

Lady Truckers rout the Black Scorpions

They score a dozen runs; pull into a tie for first place

LPGA hosts third youth clinic ahead of Pure Silk Bahamas LPGA Classic

BGF looking to shake elitist reputation

Guardian

PM against gay marriage

But Christie won't speak for govt on issue

TRAVIS CARTWRIGHT-CARROLL
Guardian Staff Reporter
travis@nasguard.com

Published: Mar 12, 2013

Prime Minister Perry Christie said yesterday he does not believe in same-sex marriage and it is not an issue on the government's agenda.

A few weeks ago, Chief Justice Sir Michael Barnett predicted that the Bahamian courts will soon have to address the question of same-sex marriage.

When asked his reaction to the issue, Christie said: "For me it never arose.

"It's something I don't believe in. It's something that would never have come up with me, and it doesn't come up.

"It's a matter that one has to understand that exists in other countries next to us.

"It has become the law in some countries and we have to respect the laws of the countries.

"But when it comes to The Bahamas there's no issue before my government about changing the laws with respect to marriage."

Anglican Bishop Laish Boyd recommended to the Constitutional Commission last month that the constitution be amended to reflect that no one should be discriminated against based on sexual orientation.

Boyd, however, said he does not believe same-sex marriage should be included.

Human rights activist Erin Greene later recommended to the commission that homosexuals have the right to marry in The Bahamas.

When asked if he would consider including the question on the government's upcoming constitutional referendum, Christie said the government would have to decide.

"I can only speak for myself personally," he said.

"On all matters to do with conscience a government has to decide on it and I'm not going to speak for my government.

"This happened when the laws were changed to allow homosexuality in private with consenting adults, and so again it was a matter of conscience with people voting.

"It's just one of those issues that have come up and I heard [Fox Hill MP Fred Mitchell] speak this morning about the human rights position, when we took the position that we were against discriminating and violence on it and people drew inferences from that.

"I don't see it as an issue in The Bahamas today. I don't see it as an issue before my government. It most certainly is not an issue before my government."

Christie was referring to a vote by the United Nations to support the rights of the lesbian, gay, bisexual, and transgender (LGBT) community.

In the House yesterday, Mitchell said Christie's support of the resolution caused a "ripple, perhaps even in our own party".

"But the rationale was this: How could The Bahamas, a nation of majority black people...victims of discrimination, prejudice and violence, support a resolution which if passed in the negative could mean that The Bahamas supported violence against people," Mitchell said.

Mitchell defends

In his contribution in the House, Mitchell also outlined what he said were personal attacks made against him for his support of LGBTs.

"When I spoke last in this place, I made a passing reference to my support for the rights of LGBT people as far back as 1978," he said.

"That has now become the subject of an assault on my reputation which is an example of the kind of prejudice at work in the country which is the kind that cannot be outlawed, but which exists all the same.

"I have no doubt that the public commentary that uttered forth from a pulpit about that one reference was designed to sully my character and to prejudice people against me.

"It is quite sad.

"At the age of 59 I say again, do not confuse politeness and civility for weakness."

This content has been locked. You can no longer post any comment.

Guardian

search... | Search

The march to gay marriage

Church stands strong in its opposition to changing marriage laws

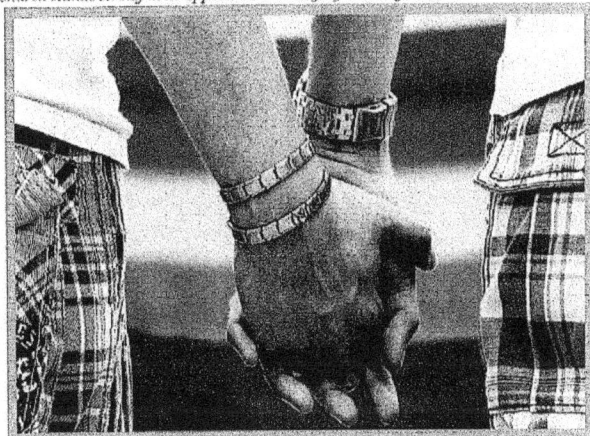

The church stands strong in its opposition to same-sex marriage. AP

TANEKA THOMPSON
Guardian Senior Reporter
taneka@nasguard.com

Published: Feb 21, 2013

Most people are lucky enough to have experienced the thrill of falling in love – that rush of butterflies in your stomach when the person who has captured your heart is near.

Over time those feelings often are the foundation of the desire to spend a lifetime together in marriage.

Share This:

Rate this article:

Remove From Favourite

However, for gay and lesbian couples in jurisdictions such as The Bahamas, there is no path to matrimony.

Weeks after the controversial gambling referendum debate ended the question of legalizing gay marriage emerged.

Last Friday, Chief Justice Sir Michael Barnett told a crowd of lawyers that he thinks Bahamian courts will soon have to address the issue of same-sex marriages. Sir Michael referenced the changing perception of gay marriage in countries such as Canada, the United States and Britain. Consequently, he said he expects that Bahamians will soon have to look at the issue. Gay marriage is not legal in The Bahamas.

"Ours is an ever shrinking global village," Sir Michael said. "The problems that affect the lives of our citizens and the residents of our respective countries have more in common than there are differences.

"Our respective countries both have written constitutions that protect our human rights. Our citizens and visitors look to us, the justices of court, to protect these rights. Little justice is served by reinventing the wheel."

Members of the religious community have responded to those comments. They have vowed to fight any measure to legalize same-sex marriage.

"The worldwide encroachment of lesbians and homosexual lifestyles against heterosexuality will only be curtailed or derailed by greater emphasis on strong functional loving family life," said Bishop Simeon Hall, retired senior pastor of New Covenant Baptist Church, in an interview.

"The homosexual community is, in my opinion, the fastest growing sub-culture in our Bahamas and indeed in the world. While some persons choose a gay or lesbian lifestyle, some studies show that most practicing homosexuals come from dysfunctional families. Strong, loving functional families are the last bastion against the homosexual avalanche.

"Spousal abuse, incest and rape, all these have irreversible negative effects on children and unfortunately and regrettably these are on the rise and I believe the root cause of homosexuality. The short-term response to this avalanche is to first affirm that homosexuals and gays are first human-beings. While I affirm that homosexuals are yet humans, I also assert that the practice is a deviance from what God's word has established."

A homosexual Bahamian man who left the country several months ago to marry his long-time love recently told The Nassau Guardian that The Bahamas needs to follow the lead of countries that have legalized same-sex marriage.

Mindell Small, who was an equal rights activist while he lived in New Providence, recently married his male partner. Same sex marriages are legal in Canada where Small now lives with his husband.

Small said he does not intend to move back to The Bahamas because of the discrimination he faced because of his sexual orientation. However, he added that he and his husband intend to purchase a vacation home on one of the Family Islands.

Despite the hostility to homosexuals in the country at this time, Small thinks same-sex marriage will happen eventually.

The Bahamas Christian Council (BCC) stance against gay marriage is not fueled by bigotry, according to one of its senior members.

"This has nothing to do with us being homophobic. It has nothing to do with that. It has everything to do with the idea that marriage is God's idea and we don't want anyone to dilute that," said BCC Vice President Rev. Victor Cooper.

This content has been locked. You can no longer post any comment.

The Atlantic

Christian and LGBT Groups Have Brought the Battle for Gay Rights to the Caribbean

Controversy over the region's colonial-era "buggery" laws is exposing a new form of advocacy -- and anti-colonialism.

JAVIER CORRALES AND CAMERON COMBS | JUN 27, 2013

Opponents of a gay rights bill gather in Guyana in 2003. (AP)

After two young men were seen having sexual intercourse in a university bathroom in Jamaica last year, they were set upon by a mob, who cheered as security guards kicked, punched, and slapped one of the boys. The attack was yet another sign that homophobia is alive and well in many Caribbean nations.

The West is known for exporting its culture, but also its culture wars. The fight for gay rights abroad is the latest example. Powerful, U.S.-based Christian-conservative groups and a network of pro-LGBT transnational actors have each become deeply involved in debates about homosexuality in many countries of the Global South.

Today, criminal bans on sodomy still exist in a whopping 78 countries, many holdovers from British colonialism.

These gay "proxy wars" are especially intense in former English colonies. These territories are inheritors of an acute obsession with sexual puritanism, which is evident in how their laws treat homosexuality. Convinced that native societies were morally corrupt and licentious, colonial governments and pastors prescribed harsh laws against same-sex relations in British territories. These "buggery" statues became a colonial mainstay in the 19th century. Originally, these laws banned any form of "unnatural connection," including bestiality, but their lasting impact has been the criminalization of male homosexuality. Today, criminal bans on sodomy still exist in a whopping 78 countries, many holdovers from British colonialism.

But 200 years later, change is starting to take root. Even in the most intolerant places, local actors have emerged to revoke these laws. Needless to say, they face formidable opponents.

International actors have passionately joined these foreign battles. For supporters of LGBT rights in the Global North, the myriad injustices that the world's sexual minorities suffer equate to grave human rights violations. Some European nations, and now even the U.S. State Department, have made LGBT-protection an important part of their objectives abroad.

For conservative religious organizations, mostly in the United States, foreign countries represent not just a fresh opportunity to influence the debate over homosexuality, but also a source of fundraising and followers. Even before the June 26 Supreme Court rulings on gay marriage in the United States, these groups recognized that they were losing the gay-rights debate at home, but they figure that their chances are better abroad.

The Anglophone Caribbean is a prominent example of this exported culture war -- sodomy bans exist in 11 Caribbean nations. Although though these buggery laws are hardly ever enforced, they give credence to actors who promote intolerance. From openly homophobic artists to tourist officials resistant to gay visitors, the English-speaking Caribbean is no gay paradise.

The good news is that these laws are no longer taken for granted. In 2011, the current prime minister of Jamaica campaigned promising to end buggery laws. On June 25 this year, the Jamaican Supreme Court heard a complaint against the nation's buggery laws. That case paralleled another petition to repeal Jamaica's law before the Inter-American Commission on Human Rights (IACHR). In May, the Belizean Supreme Court tried a challenge to Section 53 of its criminal code, which condemns "carnal intercourse against the order of nature" with 10 years in prison. Later that month, the prime minister of Dominica was compelled to weigh in on the debate in his own country, asserting that repeal of the sodomy ban was out of the question for the "foreseeable future." A few days later, newspapers in Grenada published a letter from the president of the senate urging a review of the island's buggery law. Similar legal challenges to sodomy bans have occurred this year in several other former British colonies - Singapore, India, and Northern Cyprus.

The bad news is that these folks are fighting not just local mores, but also a large battalion of U.S. churches and church-related groups siding with the defenders of the status quo.

Many of these small Caribbean nations frequently host Phillip Lee, director of the California-based religious organization His Way Out Ministries, which has ties to Focus on the Family. Lee, a man who says he's formerly gay and has renounced "the lifestyle," preaches that prayer can reverse same-sex attractions. He has met with high-level officials such as the governor general of Jamaica and the mayor of Port of Spain, the capital of Trinidad and Tobago. In his words, "the Caribbean is ripe for ex-gay ministry planting and development." In March of this year, Lee traveled to Guyana (which he claims to have visited some 20 times) as well as to Trinidad and Tobago. In both counties, he made several radio and television appearances, hosted well-attended workshops, and publically expressed support for keeping sodomy bans on the books. In Belize, the most prominent advocate of maintaining the country's buggery law is Scott Stirm, a Texan emigre and the founder of Belize Action, the main organization opposing the effort to decriminalize sodomy. As *The Economist* recently reported, Stirm's efforts are buoyed by support from the Alliance Defending Freedom, an Arizona-based religious advocacy organization.

Pro-LGBT international advocacy groups have sought to contain this crusade.

Their strategy has largely hinged on the inclusion of LGBT issues within the human rights agenda of multilateral forums, such as the IACHR and prominent NGOs. AIDS-Free World, based in New York City, filed the challenges against Jamaica's buggery laws, both before the Jamaican Supreme Court and the IACHR. It has also launched a lawsuit against two Jamaican TV stations and the Corporation for Public Broadcasting of Jamaica (PBCJ) over their refusal to air a pro-gay PSA, and is also challenging the travel ban on homosexuals in Belize and Trinidad and Tobago. In Belize, the Human Dignity Trust, the International Commission of Jurists, and the Commonwealth Lawyers Association have all joined the fray as interested parties in support of the complainant. Their representation includes Lord Peter Goldsmith, former attorney general for England and Wales.

**

Domestically, these international influences are generating backlash. A visit to Trinidad and Tobago by Phillip Lee in 2010 provoked, in the words of the country's most prominent gay rights organization, "the largest (and perhaps the first) GLBT protest in T&T's history." Young people, galvanized by the harmful effects that reparative therapy has had on their counterparts in the United States, organized the gatherings to challenge Lee's "message of exclusion and conversion." One organizer cited the elevated rates of suicides among LGBT youth in the United States as grounds to resist the ex-gay movement in Trinidad and Tobago.

At the same time, critics of LBGT rights have assumed a hyper-nationalist position, decrying international LGBT groups for importing their "foreign models." Advertisements in Belize, for instance, have sought to portray the case before the country's Supreme Court as an example of moral decadence being dragged into Belize by Barack Obama (see here, here, or here). Prior to the arguments before the Supreme Court, protestors in Jamaica lambasted the buggery case as emblematic of the attempt by gay rights advocates to "take over the world."

Local conservative groups have thus turned the debate about gay rights into a debate against neocolonialism. The paradox is that some of these groups decry interventionism even though they themselves are welcoming anti-gay Christian movements from abroad.

International pro-LGBT rights group thus have perplexing problem on their hands: helping local actors fight against transnational Christian forces while at the same time protecting themselves from accusations of neocolonialism. It seems that aid from religious groups is not subject to the same imperialist stigma, not to mention the fact that buggery laws themselves were imposed on Caribbean societies from outside.

Conditionality could become one way to fight the status quo. Foreign stakeholders are beginning to require countries to adopt friendlier gay policies in exchange for, in this case, tourist dollars or foreign aid. When the Grenadian president of the senate urged a review of the anti-sodomy law, a principal reason he gave was that wealthier nations could impose sanctions on the island as punishment for not doing so. AIDS-Free world, meanwhile, claims its petition before the IACHR is intended to shame Jamaica, thereby imperiling tourist revenues.

But these approaches can also be counterproductive. They risk placing local LGBT populations in an antagonistic position vis-à-vis society, as they stand to shoulder the blame for sanctions intended to punish homophobic lawmakers.

Colin Robinson, executive director of a gay rights organization based in Trinidad and Tobago, asserts that a model that hinges on international arbitration rather than domestic action often comes at the "expense of nurturing local political alliances, of building ownership of GLBT issues by other sexual rights stakeholders, of developing strategic power domestically, ... or simply of being politically innovative in response to local conditions." For example, Jamaica's main LGBT organization has sought to stem international boycotts of dancehall music. While this genre has been marked by virulently homophobic rhetoric in the past, local activists worry that foreign boycotts unwittingly punish reformed artists and alienate gay rights activism from an important component of national culture.

International pro-LGBT groups could also focus more on on-the-ground objectives - such as reducing school bullying, homelessness, workplace discrimination, police and teacher sensitivity training, scholarly exchanges. Swaying public opinion, which can only be done by domestic groups, might be better than turning punitive.

In the end, there is no easy solution. Local pro-LGBT rights groups need all the help they can get, especially where it is unsafe to be openly pro-gay, as it is in many parts of the Caribbean, and this alone is an argument for continued help from abroad.

International pro-LGBT actors should thus stand ready to help, but being careful not to create new problems for the very constituencies they are trying to support. The last thing the LGBT community needs is yet another pejorative label, in the form of "Made in the USA."

BAHAMAS 2014 HUMAN RIGHTS REPORT

EXECUTIVE SUMMARY

The Commonwealth of The Bahamas is a constitutional, parliamentary democracy. Prime Minister Perry Christie's Progressive Liberal Party won control of the government in May 2012 elections that international observers found generally free and fair. Authorities maintained effective control over the security forces.

The most serious human rights problems were police abuse; mistreatment of irregular migrants (compounded by problems in processing them); and an inefficient judicial system, resulting in trial delays and an increase in retaliatory crime against both witnesses and alleged perpetrators.

Other human rights problems included substandard detention conditions; corruption; violence and discrimination against women; sexual abuse of children; and discrimination based on ethnic descent, sexual orientation, or HIV status.

The government took action against police officers and other officials accused of abuse of power.

Section 1. Respect for the Integrity of the Person, Including Freedom from:

a. Arbitrary or Unlawful Deprivation of Life

There were no reports that the government or its agents committed arbitrary or unlawful killings. There were occasional reports of fatal shootings and questionable deaths of suspects in police custody. Bystanders at some shootings claimed that police were too quick to use their firearms and, in some instances, declared that police officers acted unprofessionally.

Authorities reported five fatalities in police operations in 2013. The government did not provide updated data.

In April witnesses accused police officers of beating and kicking a 34-year-old man who later succumbed to his injuries. The Coroner's Court ruled this a wrongful death, and one officer was placed on administrative leave. The case remained pending as of October 20.

BAHAMAS

In 2011 the Coroner's Court resolved 1,278 cases and faced a backlog of 846 cases, including a few pending cases involving police shootings. The government did not provide updated data.

b. Disappearance

There were no reports of politically motivated disappearances.

c. Torture and Other Cruel, Inhuman, or Degrading Treatment or Punishment

The constitution prohibits torture and cruel, inhuman, or degrading treatment or punishment. At times citizens and visitors alleged instances of police abuse of criminal suspects.

In April 2013 a defense attorney accused a police officer of beating her client until he confessed to a 2010 murder. She further alleged that the only evidence linking her client to the crime was his disputed confession. The government did not provide updated data.

Prison and Detention Center Conditions

Prison and detention center conditions failed to meet international standards in some areas, and conditions at the government's only prison remained harsh due to overcrowding. During the year, however, prison sanitation improved. New correctional services legislation, which entered into force in August, renamed Her Majesty's Prison "The Bahamas Department of Correctional Services" (DCS); the new law places greater emphasis on rehabilitation of offenders.

Physical Conditions: DCS facilities include the remand center, remand court, maximum-security blocks, medium-security blocks, minimum-security/work release units, and a separate women's unit. Overcrowding, sanitation, and access to adequate medical care remained problems in the men's maximum-security block. In October authorities reported the daily population of the prison and the remand center at 1,396, compared with 1,433 in October 2013. To address overcrowding in the remand center, which stemmed from processing backlogs within the judicial system, authorities held prisoners awaiting trial in the maximum-security block. In October the commissioner of corrections (formerly the prison superintendent) reported the maximum-security wing of the prison held 753 inmates, which was twice the number of inmates it was built to hold when

BAHAMAS

constructed in 1953. Authorities generally held remanded non-Bahamian citizens in the maximum-security block if they were deemed to pose an escape risk. Authorities estimated that 47 percent of those held in maximum security were awaiting trial.

In October authorities reported confining as many as five inmates to cells intended for one or two prisoners. The majority of cells had adequate sanitary facilities, and additional improvements were underway as of October. Authorities allowed maximum-security inmates outside for exercise four days a week for one hour per day. Medium-security and minimum-security units had running water and toilets and, in some cases, a television set for prisoners to watch. Food supplies were adequate. A few cells, however, lacked running water, and in those cells inmates removed human waste by bucket. Four reverse-osmosis units installed at various prison housing units allowed each inmate to extract one gallon of potable water during exercise time each day, free of charge. In addition inmates could purchase bottled water and other beverages from the prison commissary.

Prison guards complained about the lack of a full-time dentist, failure to appoint a staff psychiatrist, and perimeter walls being incomplete for more than six years.

There were two inmate deaths through October. Authorities reported one was due to natural causes, and the second remained under investigation as of October.

Authorities held female prisoners at the DCS in a separate building located away from the retention area for male prisoners, but still within the same area surrounded by the prison wall. On October 1, there were 44 female prisoners. Conditions for women were less severe and less crowded than for men. Women had access to the same work-release programs available to men.

Authorities kept all juvenile offenders separated from adult offenders, holding remanded male juveniles in a custody block designated for juveniles only. They placed sentenced male juveniles at the medium security facility at the DCS and kept all female juveniles at the Female Housing Security Unit separated from adults.

The capacity of the Carmichael Road Immigrant Detention Center was 150 persons housed in two dormitories. The highest occupancy at the detention center through November was 498 persons; the population was 265 as of November 5. The dormitories were segregated by gender and secured using locked gates, metal fencing, and barbed wire. When the dormitories exceeded maximum capacity,

BAHAMAS

detention center staff utilized the floor of the main hall in the medical building to accommodate up to another 50 individuals with sleeping space. Any additional detainees slept outside. Following the implementation of the new immigration policy on November 1 (see Pretrial Detention below), authorities initially held accompanied children together with their mothers in the women's dormitory at the detention center, but later identified a local church facility where they housed the women with their children. They held unaccompanied minors in the Children's Emergency Hostel and the Elizabeth Estates Children's Home.

In September a small group of Cuban detainees attempted to set fire to the facility, reportedly to protest living conditions. Authorities reportedly contained the protest without incident, and no persons were charged. Authorities reported only minor complaints from detainees during the year, mostly concerning type and quantity of food. An advocacy group alleged that guards occasionally assaulted detainees. Human rights organizations also reported that rats and mice infested the living quarters. Some former detainees alleged that they were not allowed to contact their respective embassies or consulates. None of the eight pay telephones were operational, but detainees commonly had access to smuggled cell phones. Migrant detainees did not have access to an ombudsman or other means of submitting uncensored complaints.

The government made progress in its case against five Royal Bahamas Defence Force (RBDF) marines who in 2013 allegedly beat five Cuban detainees with batons and pipes at the Carmichael Road Immigrant Detention Center. The closed military tribunal hearing the case heard testimony on several occasions from key witnesses, several of whom traveled from Cuba and other countries to testify. In July the tribunal temporarily suspended the case while it sought testimony from one final witness abroad.

Administration: Recordkeeping was adequate. Prisoners and detainees generally had reasonable access to visitors and could participate in religious observance. Some organizations providing aid, counseling, education services, and religious instruction had regular access to inmates. A designated ombudsman was available to inmates charged with serious offenses, and other prisoners were entitled to an audience with the commissioner or a designee upon request to lodge complaints. The commissioner was available to hear the complaints of prisoners six days per week. Authorities stated that there were 87 complaints to judicial authorities concerning situations in the prison as of October, mostly related to lack of shower time, cell temperatures, and lack of access to dental facilities. Officials stated they investigated all credible allegations. Through October 1, authorities reported 803

BAHAMAS

preliminary inquiries and investigations of staff and inmates, an increase from 22 through the same period in 2013, attributed to improved processes. Alternative sentencing for nonviolent offenders was available for juveniles and persons addicted to drugs (or substance abusers).

Independent Monitoring: Human rights organizations complained that the government did not consistently grant requests by independent human rights observers for access to the DCS, Carmichael Road Detention Center, and the two juvenile centers. The government maintained additional bureaucratic procedures for some civil society organizations to gain access to the detention center, making it difficult to visit detainees on a regular basis. These groups generally operated with independence from the government.

Improvements: Through October the DCS commissioner reported improvements to the sanitation system including the installation of toilets in the maximum security block, cell-phone jammers along with a functioning pay-phone system, perimeter fortification, additional recreational facilities, and completion of new staff quarters. The damaged roof underwent major repairs during the year. A new work-release program was initiated, and prison officers assigned to the drug rehabilitation unit were trained on treating substance use disorders.

d. Arbitrary Arrest or Detention

The constitution prohibits arbitrary arrest and detention, and the government generally observed these prohibitions, although the media occasionally reported accusations of police arresting and detaining persons arbitrarily.

Civil society organizations reported incidents of arbitrary detention by immigration officers and alleged that these officers solicited bribes to secure the release of detainees.

Government officials reported that immigrant detainees who presented a security risk were held at Bahamas Correctional Services. Nongovernmental organizations (NGOs) and media sources reported that several detainees had been held for more than one year without criminal charges.

Role of the Police and Security Apparatus

The Royal Bahamas Police Force (RBPF) maintains internal security. The small RBDF is primarily responsible for external security but also provides security at

BAHAMAS

the Carmichael Road Detention Center and performs some domestic security functions such as guarding foreign embassies. The Ministry of National Security oversees both the RBPF and the RBDF. The RBDF augments the RBPF in administrative and support roles.

Authorities automatically placed police officers under investigation if they were involved in shooting or killing a suspect. Police investigated all cases of police shootings and deaths in police custody and referred them to a coroner's court for further evaluation. The Police Complaints and Corruption Branch (PCCB), which reports directly to the deputy commissioner, is responsible for investigating allegations of police brutality or other abuse. This unit determines if enough evidence of abuse or misconduct exists in a particular case to warrant disciplinary action within the police system or, in some cases, criminal prosecution by the attorney general. The PCCB had 21 staff members to process complaints against police officers.

In addition to the PCCB, the independent Police Complaints Inspectorate Office (PCIO) investigated complaints against police. The PCIO, which is composed of five citizens, meets several times per year. No information was available on the outcome of PCIO proceedings.

From January to October 2013, there were 163 complaints against officers, half of which involved assault. Other complaints included unethical behavior, property damage, unlawful arrest, stealing, missing property, causing harm, threats of harm, neglect of duty, indecent assault, and unlawful entry or search. Of these cases authorities resolved 31 and recommended court inquiries in 13 cases. The government failed to provide updated data.

Arrest Procedures and Treatment of Detainees

In general authorities conducted arrests openly and, when required, obtained judicially issued warrants. Serious cases, including suspected narcotics or firearms offenses, do not require warrants where probable cause exists. The law provides that authorities must charge a suspect within 48 hours of arrest. Arrested persons appear before a magistrate within 48 hours (or by the next business day for cases arising on weekends and holidays) to hear the charges against them. Police can apply for a 48-hour extension upon simple request to the court and for longer extensions with sufficient showing of need. Some persons on remand claimed they were not brought before a magistrate within the 48-hour time frame. The government generally respected the right to a judicial determination of the legality

BAHAMAS

of arrests. The constitution provides the right for those arrested or detained to retain an attorney at their own expense; volunteer legal aides were sometimes available. Minors under age 18 are provided legal assistance and have the right to communicate with a parent or guardian.

There was a functioning bail system. Individuals who could not post bail were held on remand until they faced trial. Judges sometimes authorized cash bail for foreigners arrested on minor charges; however, foreign suspects generally preferred to plead guilty and pay a fine rather than pursue their right to defend themselves, in view of possible delays in court cases and harsh conditions in prison.

Pretrial Detention: Attorneys and other prisoner advocates continued to complain of excessive pretrial detention due to the failure of the criminal justice system to try even the most serious cases in a timely manner. The constitution provides that authorities may hold suspects in pretrial detention for a "reasonable period of time," which was defined as two years. As of October 20, 369 prisoners including 15 non-Bahamian citizens were awaiting trial. Authorities continued to use an electronic ankle-bracelet surveillance system in which they released selected suspects awaiting trial with an ankle bracelet on the understanding that the person would adhere to strict and person-specific guidelines defining allowable movement within the country. The chief magistrate reported that courts utilized the technical capabilities of the program appropriately, imposing curfews and geographical restrictions. In November authorities reported the monitoring of approximately 400 accused persons through the ankle-bracelet system.

Authorities detained irregular immigrants, primarily Haitians, until arrangements could be made for them to leave the country or they obtained legal status. The average length of detention varied significantly by nationality, willingness of governments to accept their nationals back in a timely manner, and availability of funds to pay for repatriation. Authorities usually repatriated Haitians within one to two weeks. In a June bilateral agreement between the governments of The Bahamas and Haiti, the Haitian government agreed to accept the return of its nationals without undue delay, and both governments agreed that Haitian migrants found on vessels illegally in Bahamian territorial waters would be subject to immediate repatriation. In return, the Bahamian government agreed to continue reviewing the status of Haitian nationals with no legal status and without criminal records who either had arrived in The Bahamas before January 1985 or had resided continuously in The Bahamas since that time. Authorities held irregular immigrants convicted of crimes other than immigration violations at the DCS

BAHAMAS

where, after serving their sentences, they often remained for weeks or months pending deportation.

On November 1, the government began enforcement of new immigration policies that clarified existing requirements for non-Bahamian citizens to carry the passport of their nationality and proof of legal status in The Bahamas. Some international organizations alleged that enforcement focused primarily on people of Haitian origin, that rights of children were not respected, and that expedited deportations did not allow time for due process. There were also reports that immigration officials physically abused persons as they were being detained and that officials solicited and accepted bribes to avoid detention or secure release. Activists for the Haitian community acknowledged that few formal complaints were filed with government authorities as a result of these allegations but attributed this to a widespread perception of impunity for police and immigration authorities and fear of reprisal among minority communities. The government denied these allegations and publicly committed to ensuring that immigration operations be carried out with due respect for internationally accepted human rights standards, including the involvement of the Ministry of Social Services, where warranted, in cases involving children, scaled enforcement based on the ability to provide adequate housing for detainees, and full investigations of any allegations of abuse.

e. Denial of Fair Public Trial

Although the constitution provides for an independent judiciary, sitting judges are not granted tenure, and some law professionals asserted that judges were incapable of rendering completely independent decisions due to lack of job security. Procedural shortcomings and trial delays were a problem. The courts have not kept pace with the rise in criminal cases, and there was a growing backlog.

Trial Procedures

Defendants enjoy a presumption of innocence until proven guilty and are permitted to question witnesses at trial and view government evidence. Defendants have a right to appeal. Defendants can elect to use a jury in criminal cases; serious offenses, such as murder and fraud, automatically go to a jury. Defendants have the right to present their own witnesses and evidence. Although defendants generally have the right to access government-held evidence and confront adverse witnesses, in some cases the law allows witnesses to testify anonymously against accused perpetrators in order to protect themselves from intimidation or retribution. Authorities frequently dismissed serious charges because witnesses

BAHAMAS

either refused to testify or could not be located. Efforts to protect witnesses were hindered by the fact that 70 percent of citizens lived within the 80 square miles that make up New Providence Island.

Defendants may hire an attorney of their choice. The government provided legal representation only to destitute suspects charged with capital crimes, leaving large numbers of defendants without adequate legal representation. Lack of representation contributed to excessive pretrial detention, as some accused lacked the means to pursue their cases toward trial.

A significant backlog of cases awaiting trial remained a problem. Delays reportedly lasted five years or more. Once cases go to trial, they were often further delayed due to poor case and court management. Examples of shortcomings included inaccurate handling or presentation of evidence and inaccurate scheduling of witnesses, jury members, and accused criminals for testimony. The government added four more criminal courts (for a total of 10) by the end of the year.

Local legal professionals attributed delays to a variety of longstanding systemic problems, such as slow and limited police investigations, inefficient prosecution strategies, limited forensic capacity, lengthy legal procedures, and staff shortages in the Prosecutor's Office and in the courts. Additional problems included a shortage of court reporters and extensive delays in producing transcripts. According to several legal professionals, government control of the budget and assignment of personnel remained a separation-of-powers problem.

Political Prisoners and Detainees

There were no reports of political prisoners or detainees.

Civil Judicial Procedures and Remedies

There is an independent and impartial judiciary in civil matters, and there is access to a court to bring lawsuits seeking damages for, or cessation of, human rights violations.

f. Arbitrary Interference with Privacy, Family, Home, or Correspondence

The constitution prohibits such actions, and the government generally respected these prohibitions.

BAHAMAS

While the law usually requires a court order for entry into or search of a private residence, a police inspector or more senior police official may authorize a search without a court order where probable cause to suspect a weapons violation or drug possession exists. There were no reports of government monitoring of private communications.

Section 2. Respect for Civil Liberties, Including:

a. Freedom of Speech and Press

The constitution provides for freedom of speech and press, and the government generally respected these rights. An independent press; a relatively effective--albeit extremely backlogged--judiciary; and a functioning democratic political system combined to promote freedom of speech and press. The independent media were active and expressed a wide variety of views without significant restriction.

Internet Freedom

There were no government restrictions on access to the internet or credible reports that the government monitored e-mail or internet chat rooms without appropriate legal authorization. The internet was widely available on New Providence and Grand Bahama islands, and the International Telecommunication Union estimated that 72 percent of the population used the internet in 2013.

Academic Freedom and Cultural Events

There were no government restrictions on academic freedom or cultural events. The Plays and Films Control Board rated and censored plays and films for public viewing.

b. Freedom of Peaceful Assembly and Association

The constitution provides for freedom of assembly and association, and the government generally respected these rights.

c. Freedom of Religion

See the Department of State's *International Religious Freedom Report* at www.state.gov/religiousfreedomreport/.

BAHAMAS

d. Freedom of Movement, Internally Displaced Persons, Protection of Refugees, and Stateless Persons

The constitution provides for freedom of internal movement, foreign travel, emigration, and repatriation, and the government generally respected these rights. The government generally cooperated with the Office of the UN High Commissioner for Refugees (UNHCR) and other humanitarian organizations in assisting refugees and asylum seekers. The government did not systematically share its prescreening notes with the UNHCR, but it sought UNHCR advice on specific cases of concern.

Protection of Refugees

Access to Asylum: The government made some improvements to its system for providing protection to refugees and asylum seekers. Trained individuals screened applicants and referred them to the Ministry of Foreign Affairs and Immigration (MFA). If approved by the MFA, applications are forwarded to the cabinet for a final decision. Authorities did not consistently seek advisory assistance from the UNHCR, but did seek advice on specific cases during the year. Those requesting asylum screening often lacked access to legal counsel. International human rights organizations reported that the government maintains a memorandum of understanding with the Cuban government allowing for information sharing that heightened the risk of the persecution of detainees and their families. From January to October 2013, the UNHCR reported 92 requests for asylum, all but one from Cuban nationals. The government recognized 12 as refugees, with some cases still pending. The UNHCR did not have consistent access to case information during the year, and the government did not provide updated data on the number of asylum requests.

Refoulement: In 2013 the government signed an agreement with the government of Cuba to expedite removal of detainees. The announced intent of this agreement was to reduce the amount of time Cuban migrants spent in detention. In some cases, however, civil society groups claimed the agreement resulted in the repatriation of migrants to Cuba without a sufficient review of pending refugee/asylum claims. As of October 20, authorities reported that they had repatriated 3,409 irregular immigrants to their home countries. That group consisted of 2,852 Haitians, 189 Cubans, and 368 from other countries.

Stateless Persons

BAHAMAS

The government has not effectively implemented laws and policies to provide certain habitual residents the opportunity to gain nationality in a timely manner and on a nondiscriminatory basis. Children born in the country to non-Bahamian parents, to an unwed Bahamian father and a non-Bahamian mother, or outside the country to a Bahamian mother and a non-Bahamian father, do not acquire citizenship at birth. At year's end the public vote on a constitutional referendum to eliminate gender-based discrimination in the transmission of citizenship remained pending until sometime in 2015, and the process of finalizing the referendum questions stalled. Following the announcement to delay the vote, the government launched an education campaign to better explain the bills included in the referendum. Bahamian-born persons of foreign heritage must apply for citizenship during a 12-month window following their 18th birthday, sometimes waiting many years for a government response. The narrow window for application, difficult documentary requirements, and long waiting times have created generations of de facto stateless persons. Some commentators believed that these restrictions particularly targeted Haitian residents in the country. According to government figures, 167 persons were granted Bahamian citizenship as of December 1. A total of 290 and 247 persons were granted citizenship in 2012 and 2013, respectively. It was not clear how many of those approved were of Haitian descent.

There were no reliable estimates of the number of de facto stateless persons. The government asserted that a number of "stateless" individuals had a legitimate claim to Haitian citizenship but refused to pursue it out of fear of deportation or loss of future claim to Bahamian citizenship. Such persons often faced waiting periods of several years for the government to decide on their nationality applications and, as a result, lacked proper documentation to secure employment, housing, access to health services, and other public facilities during this period. In addition the government announced new policies in August that further restricted the ability of some migrants to secure authorization for employment, a strategy intended to discourage further illegal immigration.

Individuals born in the country to non-Bahamian parents were eligible to apply for certificates of identity that entitled them to work and allowed access to public high school-level education and a fee-for-service healthcare insurance program. Human rights advocates criticized the health insurance program as having unrealistic payment requirements that limited widespread access. Authorities allowed individuals born in the country to non-Bahamian parents to pay the tuition rate for Bahamian students when enrolled in college and while waiting for their request for citizenship to be processed.

BAHAMAS

Section 3. Respect for Political Rights: The Right of Citizens to Change Their Government

The constitution provides citizens with the ability to change their government through the right to vote in free and fair elections, and citizens exercised this right through elections based on universal suffrage.

Elections and Political Participation

Recent Elections: Prime Minister Perry Gladstone Christie took office after his opposition Progressive Liberal Party (PLP) defeated the Free National Movement (FNM) in a general election in May 2012. The PLP won 29 of the 38 parliamentary seats, with 48 percent of the popular vote. The FNM won the remaining nine seats. Election observers from the Organization of American States and foreign embassies found the elections to be generally free and fair.

Participation of Women and Minorities: Five women served in the 38-seat House of Assembly. The prime minister appointed four women to the 21-member cabinet and five women to the 16-seat Senate, one of whom was its president. Twelve of the 21 permanent secretaries were women.

Authorities did not collect information on racial background, but there were members of minorities in prominent positions in parliament and the cabinet.

Section 4. Corruption and Lack of Transparency in Government

The law provides criminal penalties for corruption by officials; however, the government did not implement the law effectively, and officials frequently engaged in corrupt practices with impunity. There were frequent reports of government corruption during the year.

Corruption: No government agency is specifically responsible for monitoring allegations of government corruption. Such allegations are reported to the commissioner of police. When allegations of corruption are brought to the attention of the House of Assembly, it may elect to constitute an investigative committee to inquire into the matter further. It was not known whether the House of Assembly chose to do so during the year.

Financial Disclosure: The Public Disclosure Act requires senior public officials, including senators and members of parliament, to declare their assets, income, and

BAHAMAS

liabilities on an annual basis. The declaration applies to spouses and dependent family members. The government publishes a summary of the individual declarations. There is no independent verification of the submitted data, and the rate of annual submission was weak, except in election years.

Public Access to Information: As of October the government had not issued implementing regulations or taken other steps to bring the 2012 Freedom of Information Act into force. The act provides access to government information upon request from citizens and permanent residents--unless one of several exceptions related to national security, diplomatic exchanges, or the security of a prison or cabinet papers applies--and stipulates a fine of 10,000 Bahamian dollars (B$) ($10,000) for anyone who contravenes the legislation.

Section 5. Governmental Attitude Regarding International and Nongovernmental Investigation of Alleged Violations of Human Rights

A number of domestic and international human rights groups generally operated without government restriction, investigating and publishing their findings on human rights cases. Government officials usually were cooperative and responsive to their views.

Government Human Rights Bodies: A governmental commissioner with ombudsman-like duties enjoyed the government's cooperation and was considered effective.

Section 6. Discrimination, Societal Abuses, and Trafficking in Persons

The constitution prohibits discrimination on the basis of race, place of origin, political opinion, or creed, and the law prohibits discrimination based on disability. The government did not always effectively enforce these prohibitions, and the constitution and the law contain provisions that discriminate on the basis of gender. Neither the constitution nor the law addresses discrimination based on language, sexual orientation and/or gender identity, or social status.

The country consists of 700 islands and cays, 12 of which were significantly inhabited. Information in this report reflects the situation in the highly populated areas on New Providence and Grand Bahama. Limited information was available from other less-populated islands.

Women

BAHAMAS

Rape and Domestic Violence: Rape is illegal, but the law does not protect against spousal rape, except if the couple is separating, in the process of divorce, or if there is a restraining order in place. The maximum penalty for an initial rape conviction is seven years; the maximum for subsequent rape convictions is life imprisonment. In practice, however, the maximum sentence was 14 years' imprisonment. In the first 10 months of 2013, authorities reported 83 rapes and initiated 20 prosecutions. The government failed to provide updated data.

Violence against women continued to be a serious, widespread problem. The Bahamas Crisis Center (BCC) estimated that the level of domestic violence exceeded 1,200 cases annually, and the Director of Social services concurred but stated that fewer than one case in 10 resulted in police involvement. The Department of Social Services initiated a new Domestic Violence Unit in January, but the new unit had difficulty reaching victims and had processed just seven cases as of October 1. Assailants killed nine women in 2013, and the government failed to provide updated data for the year.

The law prohibits domestic violence as a crime separate from assault and battery, and the government generally enforced the law. Women's rights groups cited some reluctance on the part of law-enforcement authorities to intervene in domestic disputes. The BCC worked with police by providing them with a counselor referral service when encountering rape victims. The BCC operated a toll-free hotline in New Providence and Grand Bahama, run by trained volunteers to respond to emergency calls 24 hours a day. Governmental and private women's organizations continued public awareness campaigns, highlighting the problems of abuse and domestic violence. The Ministry of Labor and Social Development's Department of Social Services, in partnership with a private organization, operated a safe house to assist female survivors. The ministry's Bureau of Women's Affairs is responsible for promoting and protecting women's rights.

Female Genital Mutilation/Cutting (FGM/C): The law does not explicitly prohibit FGM/C, but there were no reports that it occurred.

Sexual Harassment: The law prohibits criminal "quid pro quo" sexual harassment and authorizes penalties of up to B$5,000 ($5,000) and a maximum of two years' imprisonment. There were no official reports of workplace sexual harassment during the year. Civil rights advocates complained that criminal prohibitions were not enforced effectively and asserted that civil remedies, including a prohibition on "hostile environment" sexual harassment, were needed.

BAHAMAS

Reproductive Rights: Couples and individuals generally could decide freely and responsibly the number, spacing, and timing of their children, had the information and means to do so, and had the right to attain the highest standard of reproductive health, free from discrimination, coercion, or violence. Access to family planning was universally available to persons age 18 and older and to younger persons with the consent of a parent or guardian. A government website provided information for maternal and child health-care services provided by various clinics throughout the country. Women had access to maternal health services and modern contraception. According to the most recent UN data, in 2010 skilled personnel attended 99 percent of births, and 98 percent of mothers received prenatal and postpartum care. Services were available on a nondiscriminatory basis, although some immigrants did not receive postpartum care because they had no fixed address. Individuals have access to emergency health care, including services for the management of abortion complications, although abortion is not legally permitted.

Discrimination: The law does not prohibit discrimination based on gender, and discrimination against women occurred. Women were generally free of economic discrimination, however, and the law provides for equal pay for equal work. The law does not provide women with the same right as men to transmit citizenship to their foreign-born spouses. The law also makes it easier for men with foreign spouses than for women with foreign spouses to transmit citizenship to their children. The government has proposed a constitutional referendum to correct these biases, but the process appeared stalled during the year.

Children

Birth Registration: Children born in the Bahamas to married parents, one of whom is Bahamian, acquire citizenship at birth. Those born to non-Bahamian parents, to an unwed Bahamian father and a non-Bahamian mother, or outside the country to a Bahamian mother and a non-Bahamian father do not automatically acquire citizenship. In the case of unwed parents, the child takes the citizenship of the mother. All children born in the Bahamas may make application for citizenship upon reaching their 18th birthday. There is universal birth registration, and all births must be registered within 21 days of delivery. All residents, regardless of immigration status, had free access to education and social programs.

Child Abuse: Both the government and civic organizations conducted public education programs aimed at child abuse and appropriate parenting behavior;

BAHAMAS

however, child abuse and neglect remained serious problems. The RBPF operated a hotline regarding missing or exploited children. The law provides severe penalties for child abuse and requires all persons having contact with a child they believe to have been physically or sexually abused to report their suspicions to the police.

The Ministry of Social Services reported 302 cases of child abuse through June. In addition the RBPF hotline reported 131 cases through September, including 15 reports of sexual abuse. Authorities acknowledged that the system of tracking these statistics was not reliable, and the actual number of cases was likely much higher.

The penalties for rape of a minor are the same as those for rape of an adult. While a victim's consent is insufficient defense against allegations of statutory rape, it is sufficient defense if an individual can demonstrate that the accused had "reasonable cause to believe that the victim was above 16 years of age," provided the accused was under age 18. In 2012 Social Services reported 112 of cases of adults having unlawful sexual intercourse with children age 15 and younger. The government failed to provide updated data.

Sexual exploitation of children through incestuous relationships occasionally occurred, and anecdotal reports continued to suggest that this was a particular problem outside Nassau. The Ministry of Social Services may remove children from abusive situations if a court deems it necessary. The ministry provided services to abused and neglected children through a public-private center for children, the public hospital family-violence program, and the Bahamas Crisis Center.

Early and Forced Marriage: The legal minimum age for marriage is 18, although minors may marry at 15 with parental permission. Data on rates of early marriage were not available.

Female Genital Mutilation/Cutting (FGM/C): The law does not explicitly prohibit FGM/C, but there were no reports it occurred.

Sexual Exploitation of Children: The minimum age for consensual sex is 16 years. The law considers any association or exposure of a child to prostitution or a prostitution house as cruelty, neglect, or mistreatment of a child. Additionally, the offense of having sex with a minor carries a penalty of life imprisonment. Child pornography is against the law. A person who produces it is liable to life

BAHAMAS

imprisonment; dissemination or possession of it calls for a penalty of 20 years' imprisonment.

Institutionalized Children: The Department of Social Services is responsible for abandoned children up to age 18 but had very limited resources at its disposal. There is an extensive screening process for prospective foster parents, including relatives. The government found foster homes for some children, and the government hospital or Nazareth Center housed children with physical disabilities when authorities could not find foster homes or the children needed care beyond their parents' resources. Independent human rights observers reported that the government did not consistently approve access requests to the various foster care facilities. Many of these facilities were privately run with government support.

International Child Abductions: The country is a party to the 1980 Hague Convention on the Civil Aspects of International Child Abduction. For information see the Department of State's report on compliance at http://travel.state.gov/content/childabduction/english/legal/compliance.html and country-specific information at travel.state.gov/content/childabduction/english/country/bahamas.html.

Anti-Semitism

The local Jewish community numbered approximately 200 persons. There were no reports of anti-Semitic acts.

Trafficking in Persons

See the Department of State's *Trafficking in Persons Report* at www.state.gov/j/tip/rls/tiprpt/.

Persons with Disabilities

In July the government passed the Persons with Disabilities Act, which provides for the fundamental human rights of persons with disabilities as defined in the UN Convention on Persons with Disabilities. The new law addresses issues of employment, education, and access. Under the new law, businesses and public buildings have two years to make improvements to access once implementing regulations are approved. Provisions in other legislation address the rights of persons with disabilities, including a prohibition of discrimination on the basis of disability. Although the previous law mandated access for persons with physical

BAHAMAS

disabilities in new public buildings, authorities rarely enforced this requirement, and very few buildings and public facilities were accessible to persons with disabilities. The Education Act affords equal access for students, but only as resources permit, with this decision made by individual schools. On less-populated islands, children with learning disabilities often sat disengaged in the back of classrooms because resources were not available.

The Disability Division within the Ministry of Labor and Social Development reported providing the following services during the year: disability allowances to persons with disabilities; financial assistance to procure prosthetics, wheelchairs, hearing aids, and other assistive devices; regular meetings for the prosthetic committee; annual government grants to NGOs serving the community of persons with disabilities; crisis intervention counseling; and Braille classes.

A mix of government and private residential and nonresidential institutions provided education, training, counseling, and job placement services for adults and children with physical or mental disabilities.

National/Racial/Ethnic Minorities

The country's racial and ethnic groups generally coexisted peacefully, but anti-Haitian prejudice and resentment regarding Haitian immigration was widespread. According to unofficial estimates, between 40,000 and 80,000 residents were Haitians or persons of Haitian descent, making them the largest ethnic minority. Many persons of Haitian origin lived in shantytowns with limited sewage and garbage services, law enforcement, or other infrastructure. The conditions of the shantytowns varied greatly. For example, a shantytown in Abaco referred to as "the Mud" consisted of several hundred numbered houses with limited electricity, water, gas, and sewage connections. In contrast, a number of shantytowns on New Providence and other islands consisted of houses built from trash and leftover building materials, with few organizational, infrastructure, or sanitation measures in place. The government occasionally evicted residents and demolished some settlements due to health and safety concerns. Fires frequently broke out in Haitian shantytowns in Nassau, and a large fire destroyed more than 800 homes in Abaco in December 2013. Authorities generally granted Haitian children access to education and social services, but interethnic tensions and inequities persisted. The Haitian community was characterized by high poverty, high unemployment, and poor health conditions. Haitians generally had difficulty in securing citizenship, residence, or work permits.

BAHAMAS

Members of the Haitian community complained of discrimination in the job market, specifically that identity and work-permit documents were controlled by employers seeking leverage by threat of deportation. Some also complained of tactics used by immigration officials in raids of Haitian or suspected Haitian communities. Government actions to address these communities often met political resistance, as many Bahamians employed Haitians as cheap labor.

Acts of Violence, Discrimination, and Other Abuses Based on Sexual Orientation and Gender Identity

Societal discrimination against lesbian, gay, bisexual, and transgender (LGBT) individuals occurred, with some persons reporting job and housing discrimination based upon sexual orientation. According to NGOs, LGBT persons also faced discrimination in employment, for which victims had no legal recourse. The government does not keep statistics on such incidents. Although sexual activity between same-sex consenting adults is legal, the law defines the age of consent for same-sex couples as 18, compared with 16 for heterosexual couples. No domestic legislation addresses the human rights concerns of LGBT persons. LGBT NGOs could operate openly in the country, although a Pride weekend in August in Grand Bahama was nearly abandoned after organizers of the events reported receiving threats; only five persons participated. The 2006 Constitutional Review Commission found that sexual orientation did not deserve protection against discrimination.

HIV and AIDS Social Stigma

Stigma and employment discrimination against persons with HIV/AIDS were high, but there were no reports of violence against persons with HIV/AIDS. The law prohibits discrimination in employment based on HIV/AIDS status. Children with HIV/AIDS also faced discrimination, and authorities often did not tell teachers that a child was HIV positive for fear of verbal abuse from both educators and peers. The government maintained a home for orphaned children infected with HIV/AIDS.

An independent facility known as the All Saints Camp operated as a hospice for approximately 60 HIV-infected individuals, using the individuals' government and family proceeds to fund its expenses. Those in contact with the camp alleged extreme neglect of the HIV-infected individuals living at the camp, including non-nutritious and irregular meals and improper or inadequate basic medical care. The administrator of the camp reported that it did not employ nurses or other medical

BAHAMAS

staff and that sick individuals living there took care of themselves or employed their own visiting nurses. During the year several religious organizations provided physical improvements to the facility, but living conditions remained generally unsanitary.

Section 7. Worker Rights

a. Freedom of Association and the Right to Collective Bargaining

The law provides for the right of workers to form and join independent unions, participate in collective bargaining, and conduct legal strikes. The law prohibits antiunion discrimination. Under law, employers can be compelled to reinstate workers illegally fired for union activity. Members of the police force, defense force, fire brigade, and prison guards may not organize or join unions.

Enforcement of labor laws was weak. There was no information on the adequacy of enforcement resources. Fines varied widely by case and were not sufficient to deter violations. Administrative and judicial procedures were subject to lengthy delays and appeals. On October 22, the Ministry of Labor and National Insurance reported 712 labor violation complaints since January and stated that it had 16 officers who resolved the majority of these cases in a timely manner. By law labor disputes must first be filed with the ministry and if not resolved, they are transferred to an industrial tribunal, which determines penalties (fines) and remedies, up to a maximum of 26 weeks of an employee's pay. The tribunal's decision is final and can be appealed in court only on a strict question of law. Authorities reported a case backlog of up to three years at the tribunal.

Freedom of association and the right to collective bargaining were generally respected. There were reports that some employers utilized individual contracts instead of collective bargaining. An experienced trade unionist assists the ministry to streamline the collective bargaining process. Workers occasionally filed disputes with the authorities involving "union-busting" charges, specifically in the financial services sector.

b. Prohibition of Forced or Compulsory Labor

The law prohibits all forms of forced or compulsory labor, although there were reports that forced labor occurred.

BAHAMAS

The government did not always effectively enforce applicable law. Although the Ministry of Labor and National Insurance received no reports of forced labor during the year, local NGOs noted that exploited workers often did not report their circumstances to government officials for fear of deportation and lack of education about available resources. There was no information on the adequacy of resources, inspections, and remediation. Penalties for forced labor ranged from three to 10 years and were sufficiently stringent to deter violations.

Undocumented migrants were vulnerable to forced labor, especially in domestic servitude and in the agriculture sector. There were reports that noncitizen laborers, often of Haitian origin, were vulnerable to forced labor and suffered abuses at the hands of their employers, who were responsible for endorsing their work permits on an annual basis. Specifically, local sources indicated that employers reportedly obtained B$1,000 ($1,000) work permits for noncitizen employees and then required them to "work off" the permit fee over the course of their employment or otherwise risk losing the permit and their ability to work legally within the country.

Also see the Department of State's *Trafficking in Persons Report* at www.state.gov/j/tip/rls/tiprpt/.

c. Prohibition of Child Labor and Minimum Age for Employment

The law prohibits the employment of children under age 14 for industrial work or work during school hours. Children under age 16 may not work at night. Children between ages 14 and 18 may work outside of school hours under the following conditions: (a) in a school day, for not more than three hours; (b) in a school week, for not more than 24 hours; (c) in a nonschool day, for not more than eight hours; (d) in a nonschool week, for not more than 40 hours. An exception exists for "packaging boys" at grocery stores, who were as young as age 12 and may work no more than three hours after school. The law prohibits persons younger than age 18 from engaging in dangerous work including construction, mining, and road building. There was no legal minimum age for employment in other sectors. Occupational health and safety restrictions apply to all younger workers.

The government made efforts to enforce the law, with labor inspectors proactively sent to stores and businesses on a regular basis, but resource constraints limited their effectiveness. The Ministry of Labor reported no severe violations of child labor laws, although inspectors reported several instances of children working in small merchant businesses or excess hours in grocery stores. The penalty for

BAHAMAS

violations of child labor law is a fine between B$1,000 ($1,000) and B$1,500 ($1,500). This punitive action was sufficient to deter violations.

d. Discrimination with Respect to Employment or Occupation

The law prohibits discrimination in employment based on race, creed, sex, marital status, political opinion, age, HIV status, or disability, but not in regard to language, sexual orientation and/or gender identity, or social status. The government did not effectively enforce the law.

Discrimination in employment and occupation occurred with respect to persons living with HIV/AIDS (see section 6). Foreign migrant workers were not consistently afforded legal protections.

e. Acceptable Conditions of Work

Minimum wage rates exist for hourly, daily, and weekly work, but the Ministry of Labor enforces the higher minimum wage of B$4.00 ($4.00) per hour. In 2013 the official poverty level was adjusted to B$4,247 ($4,247) a year.

The law provides for a 40-hour workweek, a 24-hour rest period, and time-and-a-half payment for hours worked beyond the standard workweek. The law stipulates paid annual holidays and prohibits compulsory overtime. The law does not place a cap on overtime. The government set health and safety standards appropriate to the industries. According to the Ministry of Labor and National Insurance, the law protects all workers, including migrant workers, in areas including wages, working hours, working conditions, and occupational and safety standards. Workers did not have the right to refuse to work under hazardous conditions, and legal standards did not cover undocumented and informal economy workers.

The ministry was responsible for enforcing labor laws, including the minimum wage, and had a team of 10 inspectors that conducted on-site visits to enforce occupational health and safety standards and investigate employee concerns and complaints, although inspections occurred infrequently. The ministry generally announced inspection visits in advance, and employers generally cooperated with inspectors to implement safety standards. It was uncertain whether these inspections were effective in enforcing health and safety standards. The government did not levy fines for noncompliance, but occasionally forced a work stoppage. Such penalties were not sufficiently stringent to deter violations.

BAHAMAS

Working conditions varied, and mold was a problem in schools and government facilities.

Authorities reported no workplace fatalities from January through October.

ABOUT THE AUTHOR

Brian D. Lerner is an Immigration Lawyer and runs a National Immigration Law Firm for nearly 30 years. He is an attorney who is a certified specialist that might help in Immigration & Nationality Law as issued by the California State Bar, Board of Legal Specialization. Attorney Lerner is an expert in Immigration Law, Removal and Deportation, Citizenship, Waiver and Appeals.

He has been a licensed attorney since 1992 and started the Law Offices of Brian D. Lerner, APC. The immigration practice consists of Immigration and Nationality Law, and everything involved with and regarding immigration which includes citizenship, investment visas, family and employment visas, removal and deportation hearings, appeals, waivers, adjustment, consulate processing and all types of immigration and citizenship matters.

He has represented clients from all over the U.S. and in many countries around the world. One side of his practice is dedicated to keeping people in the U.S. and fighting for their immigration rights, while another side is to get people back who have been deported and removed from the U.S.

Also, there is the affirmative part of Immigration Law which Brian Lerner has helped numerous people come into the U.S. on business visa, investment visas, student visas, fiancee and marriage visas, religious visas and many more. Attorney Lerner has helped immigrants who are victims of crime and domestic violence or ones that are married to abusers.

In other words, Attorney Lerner has a firm that helps people all over the U.S. He has dedicated significant time to preparing numerous petitions and applications for you to get at a fraction of the price of hiring an attorney. He says it is the next best thing to a real attorney because they are real petitions prepared by an expert.

www.ingramcontent.com/pod-product-compliance
Lightning Source LLC
Chambersburg PA
CBHW051758200326
41597CB00025B/4600